Graceland Too Revisited

Images from the Home of the Universes*, Galaxys*,
Planets*, Worlds*, Ultimate #1 Elvis Fan

Photography by Darrin Devault and Tom Graves

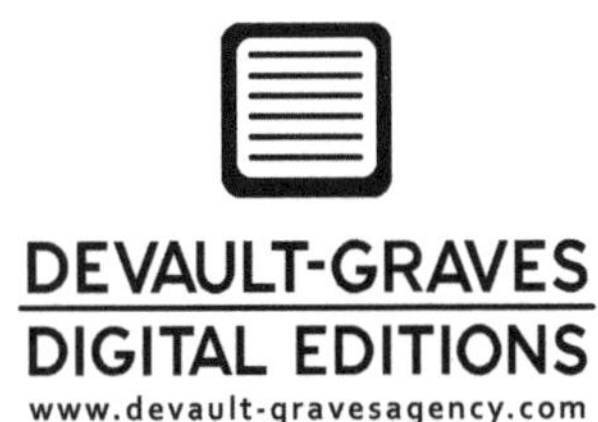

DEVAULT-GRAVES
DIGITAL EDITIONS
www.devault-gravesagency.com

ISBN: 978-1-942531-02-9

Book design and layout by Patrick Alley

*To the memory of Paul B. MacLeod,
an Elvis fan who showed us how to chase our dreams*

Graceland Too Revisited

An Introduction by Darrin Devault

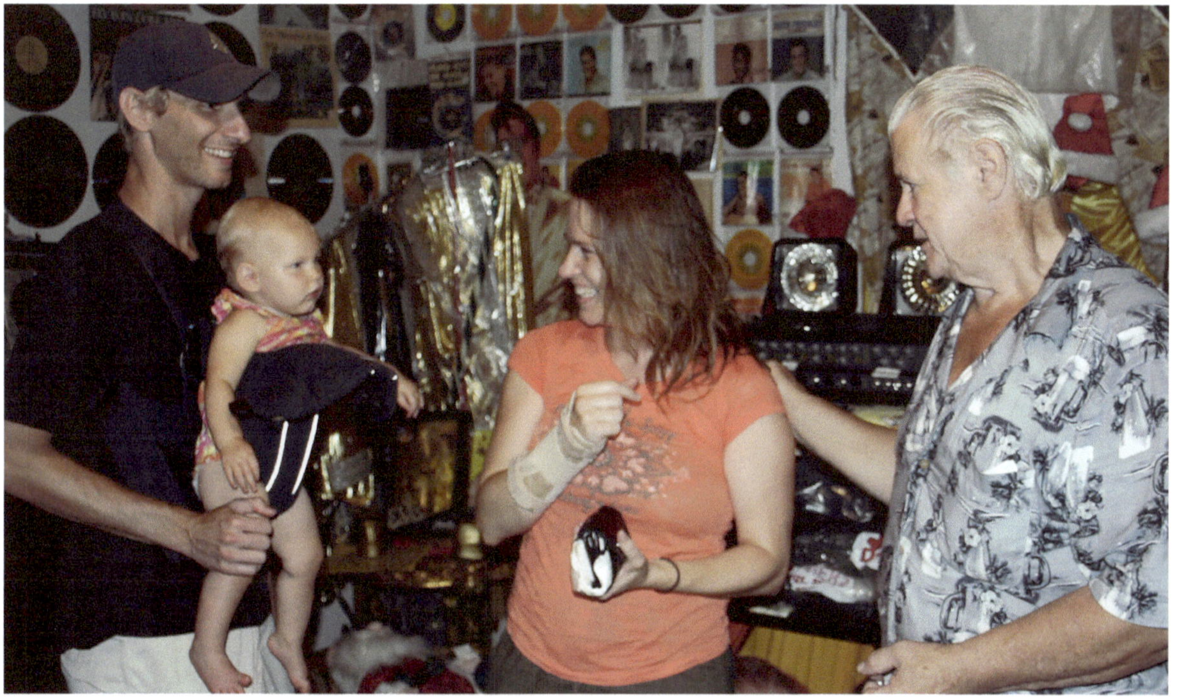

Paul B. MacLeod regaled visitors from around the world with tales about his Elvis collection.

Graceland Too, including its Elvis-obsessed owner, was a collective and organic work of Deep South folk art.

Paul B. MacLeod was the eccentric dreamer who kept his Elvis attraction open to the public round-the-clock and year-round from 1990 until his sudden death in 2014.

The location of these unforgettable curiosities was 200 E. Gholson Avenue in Holly Springs, Mississippi.

Looking back, it's difficult to determine whether the main attraction was the hot-wired Paul or the two-story antebellum home he crammed floor-to-ceiling with Elvis memorabilia, some rare (early Sun and RCA vinyl records), some made in China (velvet paintings and assorted bric-a-brac), and some handmade (an over-the-top "Jailhouse Rock" electric chair).

You could have called the entire experience a BOGO deal, because the $5 price of admission certainly had a *buy one, get one* feel to it.

My friend and photography buddy Tom Graves and I

visited Graceland Too on a muggy July afternoon in 2011, eager to capture some images of this infamous roadside attraction that somehow drew visitors from around the world yet whose mere mention was met with an eye roll or a resigned sigh from most locals. It was during Graceland Too's blue period, meaning the entire house—roof, too!—was painted blue. (Paul apparently changed the house's color scheme whenever it suited him.)

Tom and I arrived to find a stooped elderly man operating a weed eater in front of the house, carefully tending to a small strip of grass between the house and the sidewalk. Two large decorative lions, painted a more menacing shade of blue, must have scared the man from trimming the small front yard, which was covered in knee-high grass and some spray-painted fake trees.

Paul casually answered our knock on the front door, his large form filling the door frame. I heard box fans blowing in a nearby room, signaling we could expect more humidity inside.

We told Paul we'd like to tour the house and asked for permission to take photographs. He knitted his eyebrows for a few seconds, took our money, and obliged our request.

I immediately went into sensory overload as we entered the foyer filled slapdash with Elvis items. The stairwell leading to the second floor (off limits to visitors, as it is at the real Graceland) was covered with Elvis bottles, busts, and figurines—top to bottom step.

Paul's disobedient dentures started rattling around in his mouth as he encroached on my personal space and launched into a well-rehearsed, animated series of tales about Elvis and his collection. I shuffled behind Tom as a precaution.

I suppose there were elements of truth in each story Paul told about his collection and its value ("It's worth *millions!*" he said without blinking.), but before we had time to consider the veracity of one tale, he'd already sped ahead to the next. I came to respect Paul as a raconteur of the highest order.

Paul proudly showed us the music room where his mother reportedly lived in the early years of the attraction. This room featured a large collection of Elvis record albums, flashing lights, a karaoke machine, and some random Christmas decorations.

Paul caught me focusing on the records rather than his stories, and he released a short shrill whistle and gently poked my forearm to recapture my attention.

I was somewhat relieved when a young couple from Ohio joined the tour with their baby. The father carried and paid attention to the baby, while Paul turned his attention to the mother.

We later learned that Paul had a passion for women of all ages, especially the legions of Ole Miss co-eds who visited Graceland Too with their fraternity dates in the wee morning hours. It was a rite of passage that occasionally riled next-door neighbor Charlie Shaw when he was rustled from a peaceful slumber.

Meanwhile, Tom and I managed to escape to the other rooms to take photos.

Another front room contained a collection of photos of Paul in his younger days, some taken not long after his career in the automotive industry. Oh, and some more random Christmas stuff.

All of the rooms at Graceland Too held a special significance to Paul, but perhaps none more so than the shrine room, which contained his personal shrine to Elvis. Mounted high on a wall was a large framed color photo of the King covered in hardware-store lettering and a few patriotic stickers. People who visited Graceland Too three times became lifetime members, and Paul would allow them to slip on a black leather jacket and take their photograph in front of his hallowed shrine.

Paul said he ordered double photo prints of each of his new lifetime members. He would display one print in his Hall of Fans, a long vertical room in the center of the house. The floor sagged and creaked beneath the weight of all those Elvis and Graceland Too fan photos.

Paul kept the other print until the lifetime member returned for another visit. At this moment, I couldn't quiet the voice inside my head: *"My gosh, I'm looking at a man who's spent thousands of dollars on film processing and paint but never a dime on Poligrip."*

The tour continued in the kitchen, where the walls were covered with messages and signs left by previous visitors to Paul. One sign stood out because it proclaimed Paul as "The Universes, Galaxys, Planets, Worlds, Ultimate #1 Elvis Fan."

Momentarily, Tom and I stepped into Paul's glorious backyard. We discovered a collection of Cadillacs (at least three) and a pink limousine. All were plastered with more hardware-store lettering.

But then we saw the quintessential piece of folk art—a custom-built electric chair (and requisite mannequin) that reminded Paul of the Elvis film "Jailhouse Rock."

The electric chair, which didn't work but was connected to a car battery to make you wonder, was usually the last stop on the Graceland Too tour. It made for a memorable photo opportunity.

And as Paul often said, "You're all out of luck. End of the line!"

* * *

Graceland Too lifetime membership card.

Paul's life took a strange and tragic turn in mid-July 2014 when he shot and killed a local man named Dwight Taylor who reportedly tried to force his way into Graceland Too.

Paul, who, like Elvis, owned guns, was not charged. But the shooting left Paul severely shaken. Two days later, unable to sleep, Paul went out to the front porch of Graceland Too and at some time went to join his idol in eternity. He apparently died of natural causes.

Tom and I returned to Holly Springs on August 12, 2014, to attend Paul's funeral service at historic Christ Episcopal Church conducted by Rev. Bruce McMillan, who proudly noted he was a lifetime member of Graceland Too.

After the service, we made the short walk to Paul's house and took a final tour, our cameras in hand. The exterior was now painted a mix of tan and white, though a section of the former blue was showing in the upper reaches.

A collection of Coke bottles and cans had been left outside as a memorial to Paul, who boasted that he drank a case of the beverage each day.

Inside, some things remained the same as our first tour, while others had been altered or enhanced by Paul before his death. Graceland Too was indeed his life's work.

The photos on the following pages were taken from our two visits to Graceland Too. We hope you enjoy the tour.

Graceland Too (Blue Period)

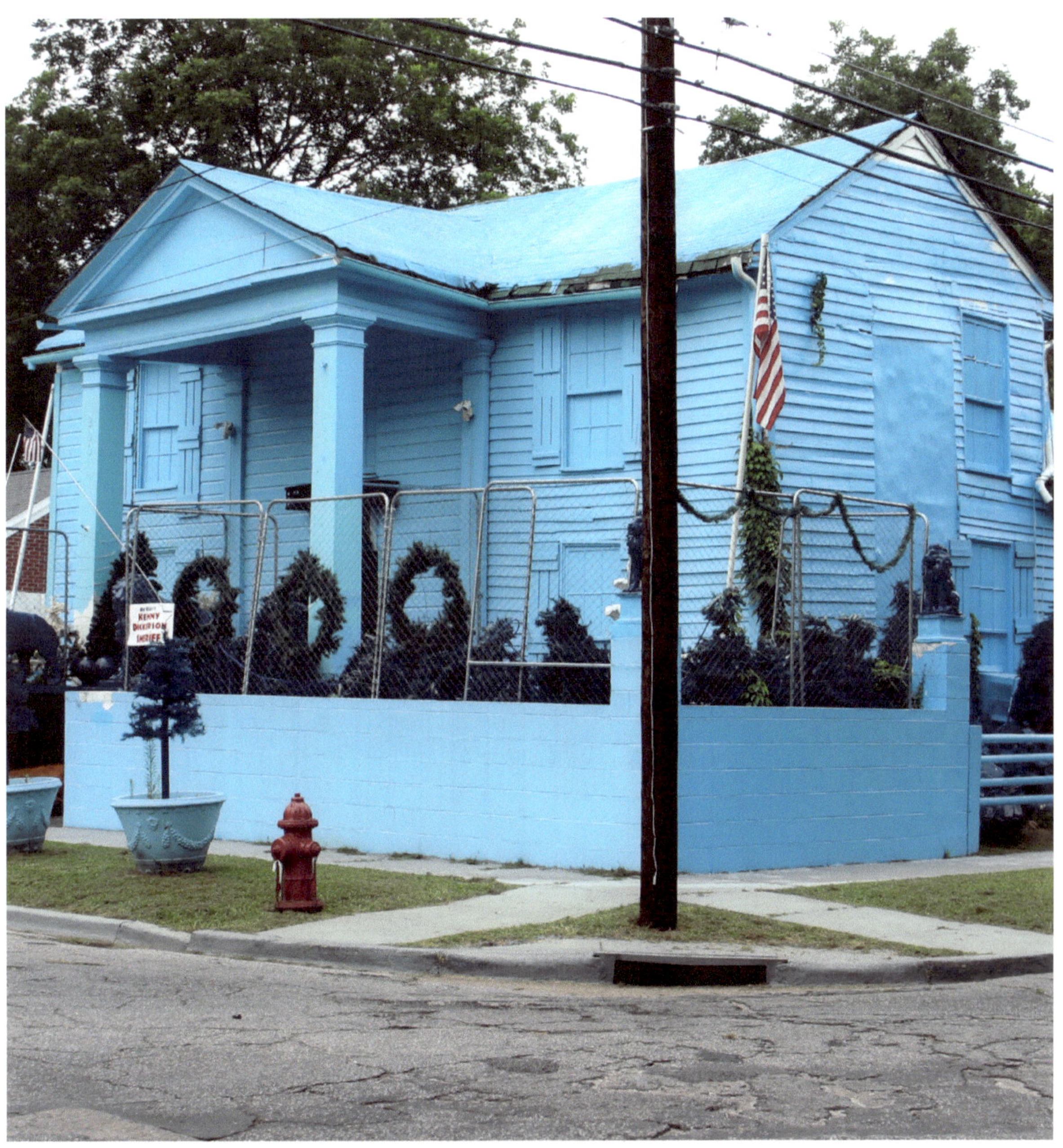KENNY
DICKERSON
SHERIFF

Blue Period Lion

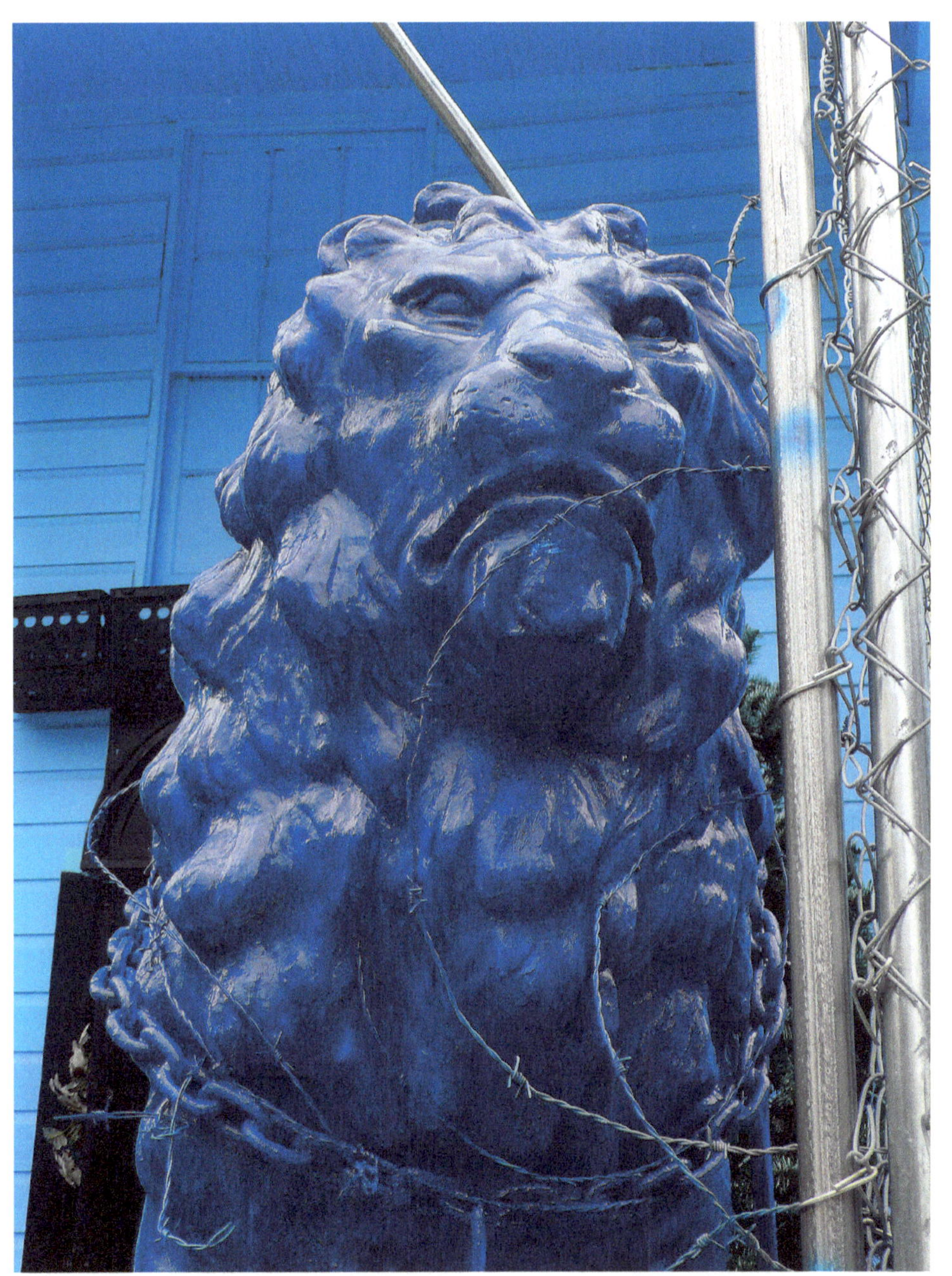

Blue Light Fixture

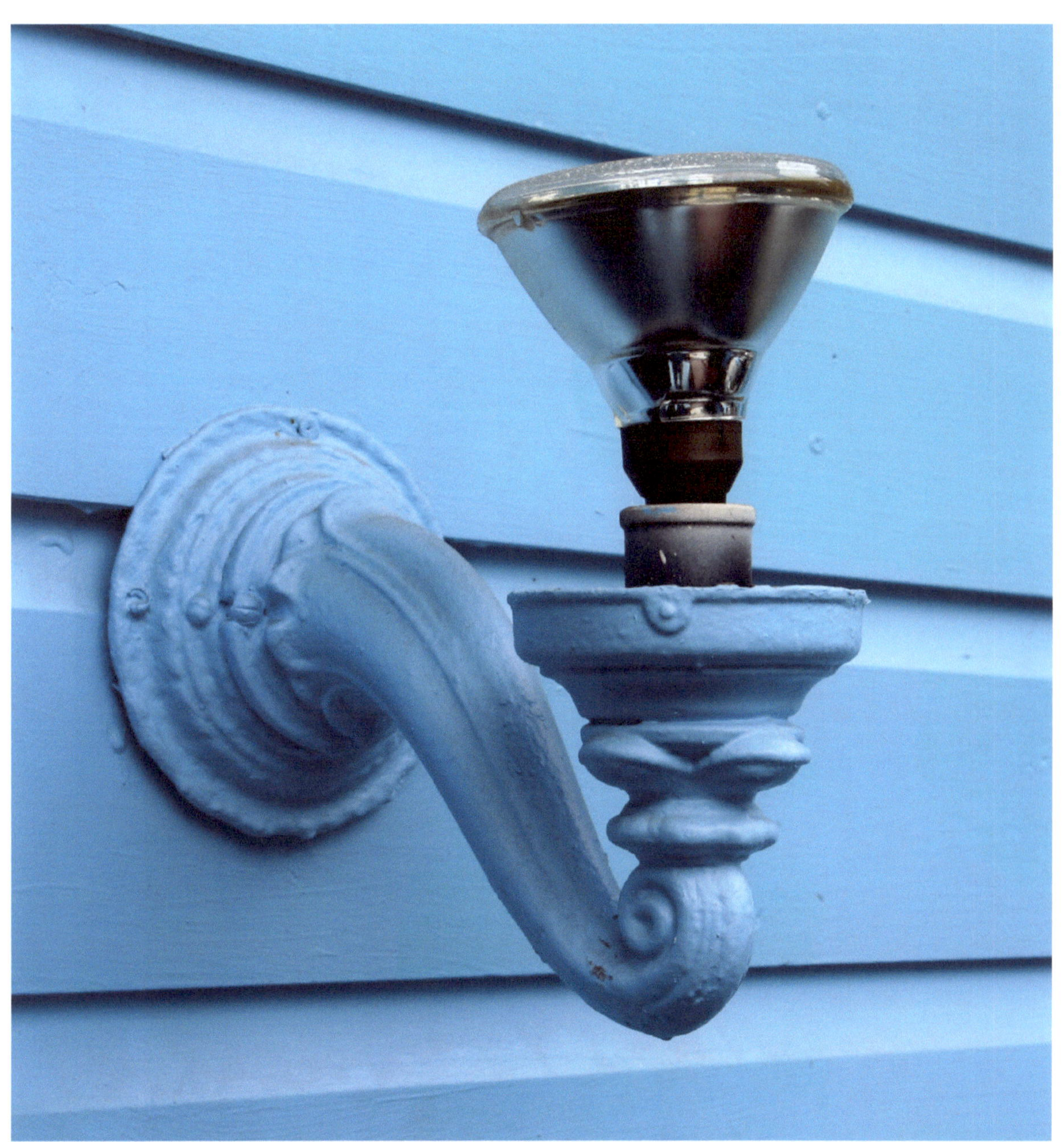

Bottles, Busts and Figurines

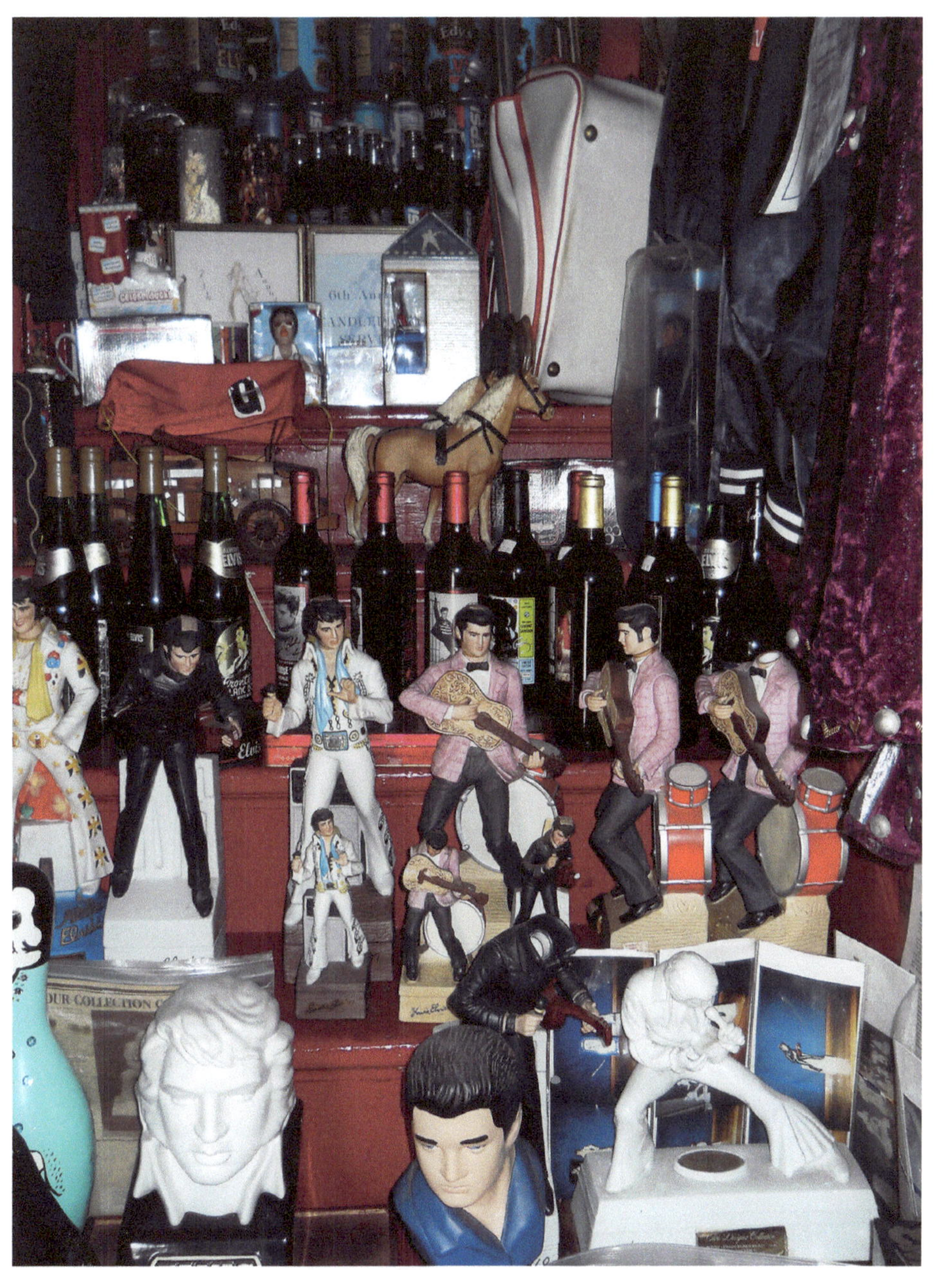

Paul Surrounded by Elvis

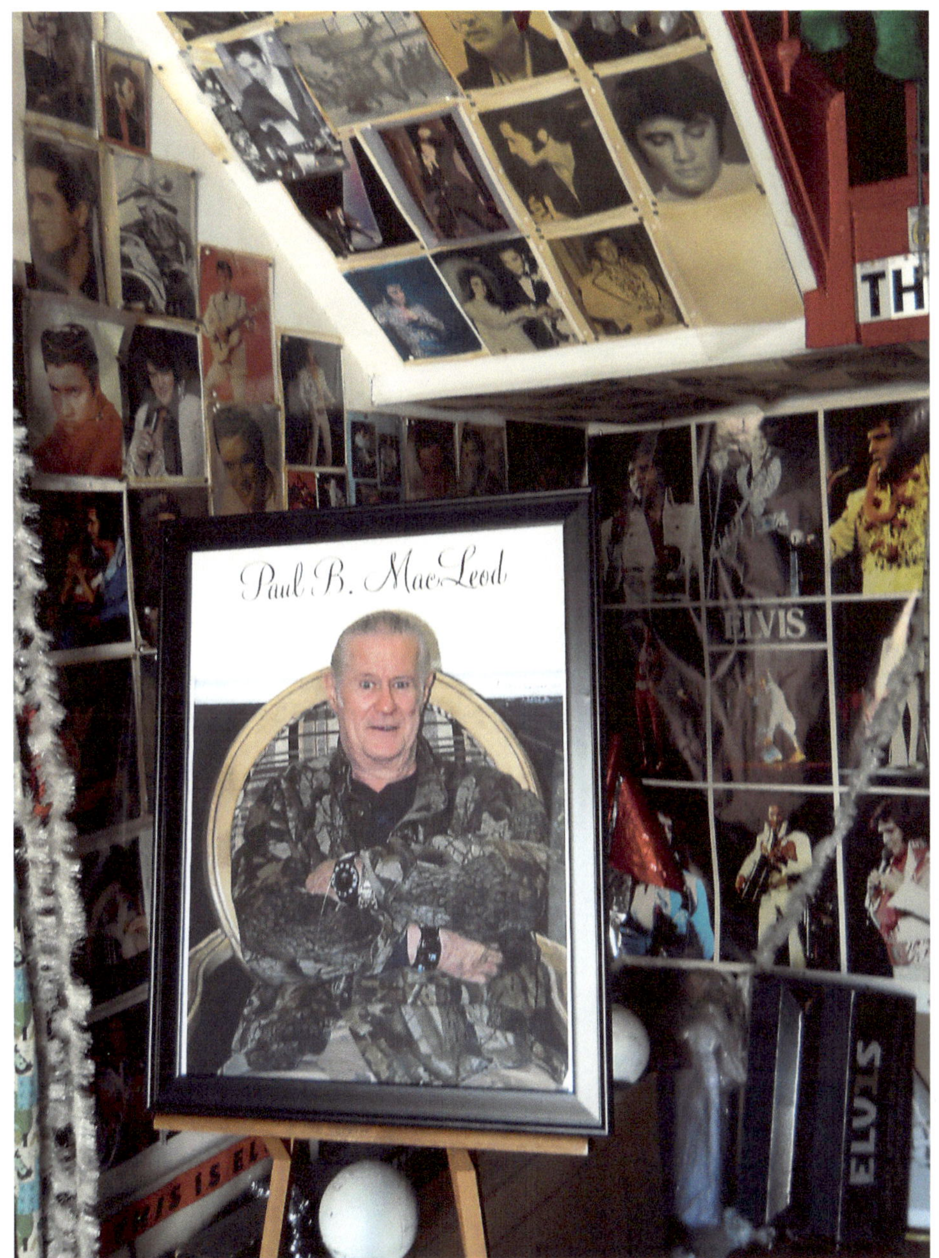
Paul B. MacLeod
ELVIS

Record Wall

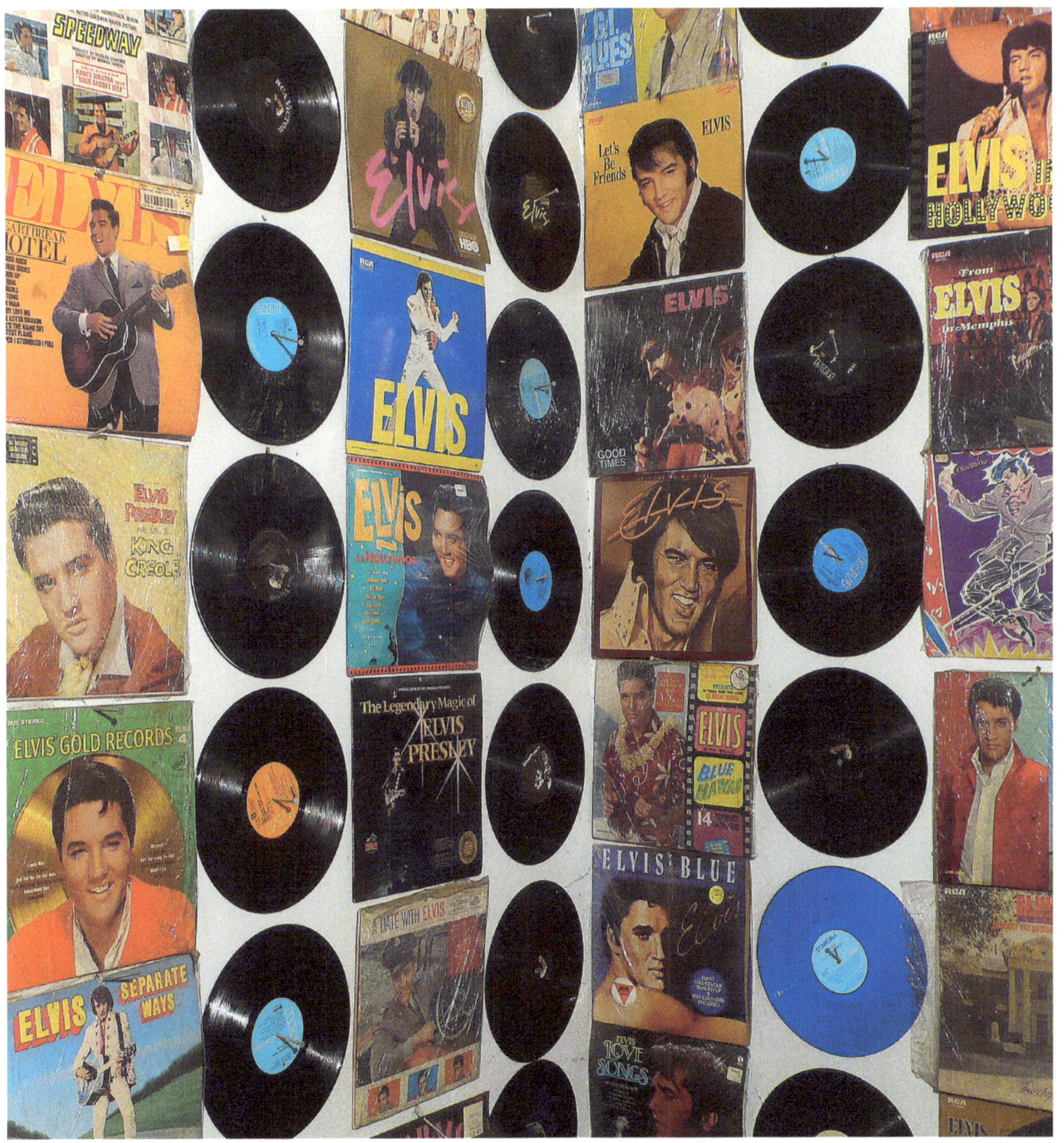

Guitar Elvis

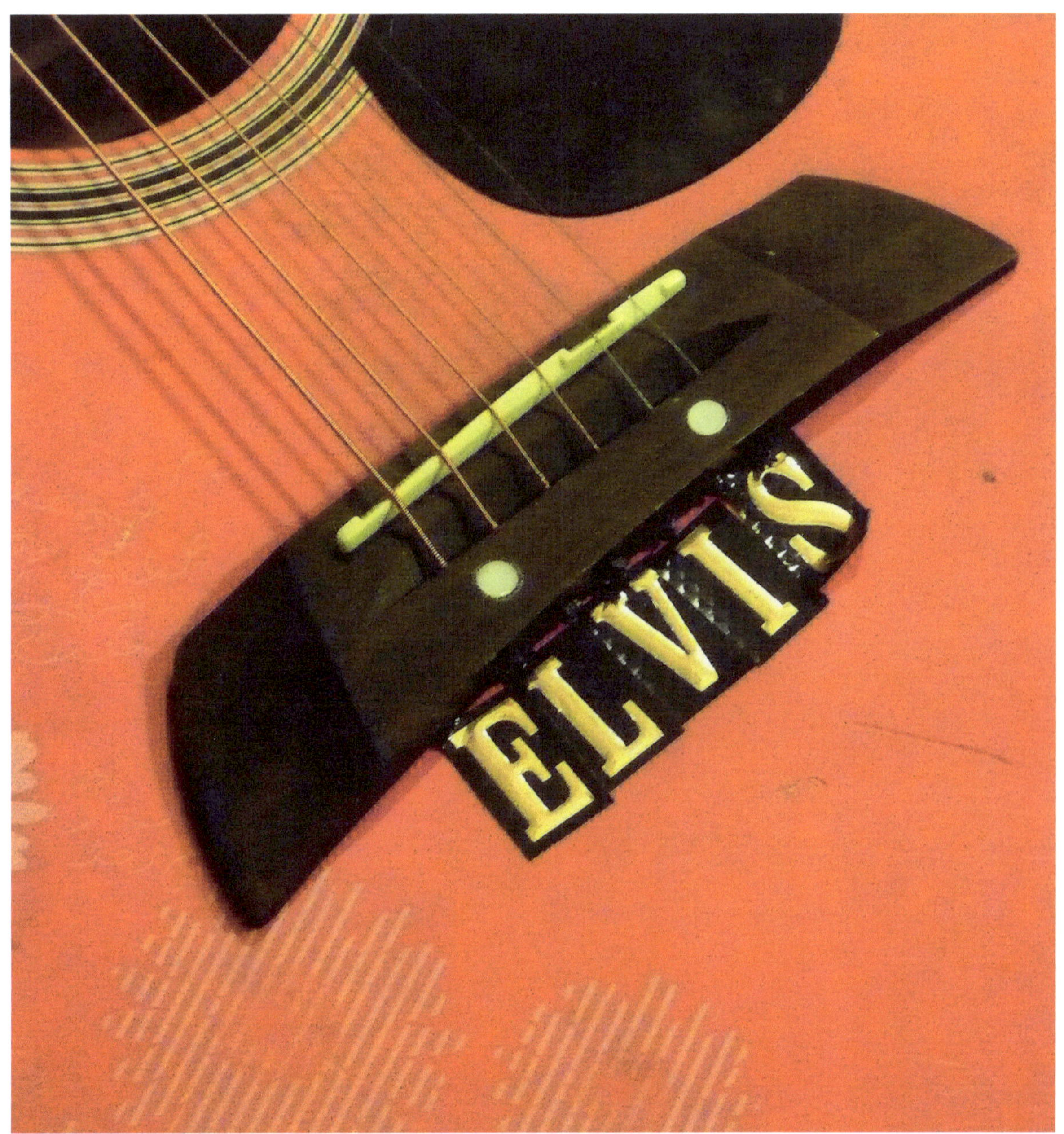

ELVIS

Elvis Door (2011)

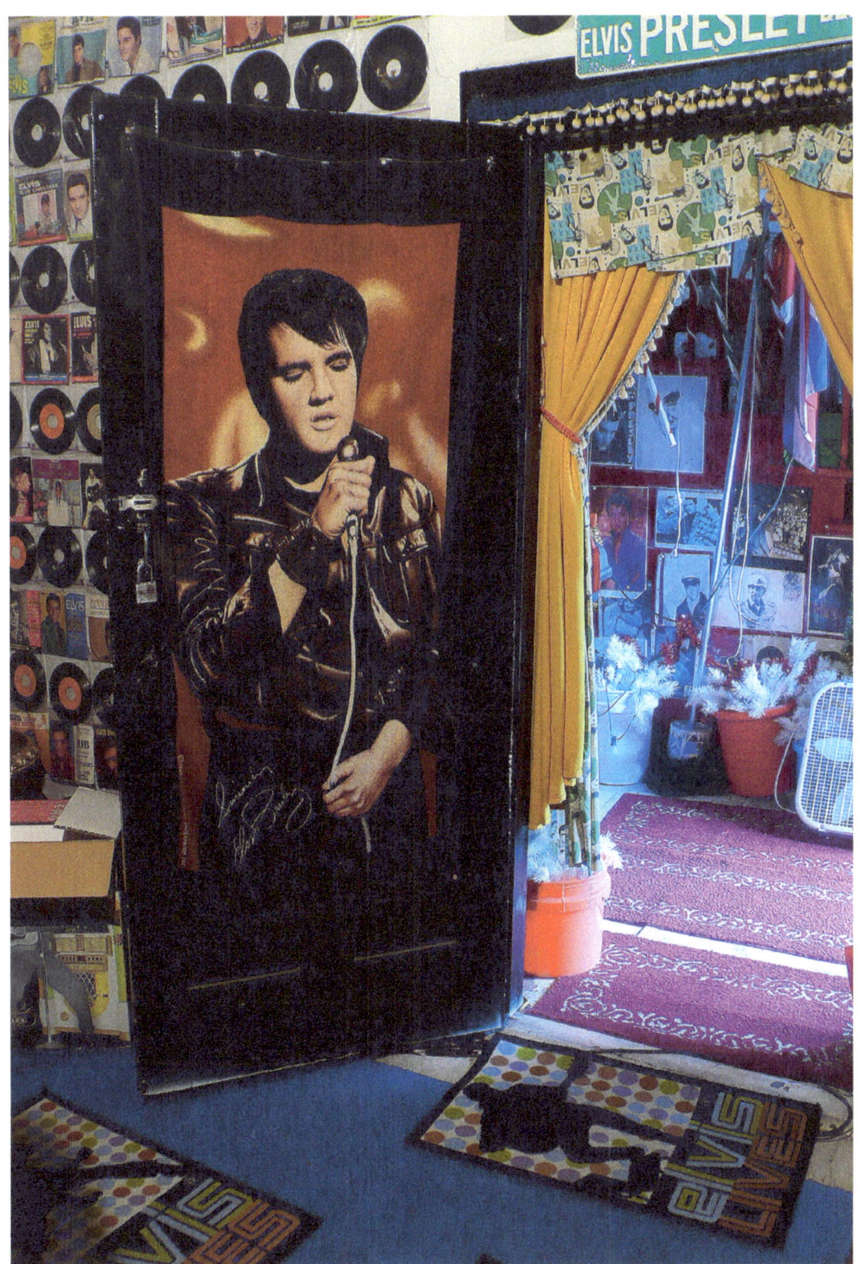
ELVIS PRESLEY
ELVIS

Elvis Door (2014)

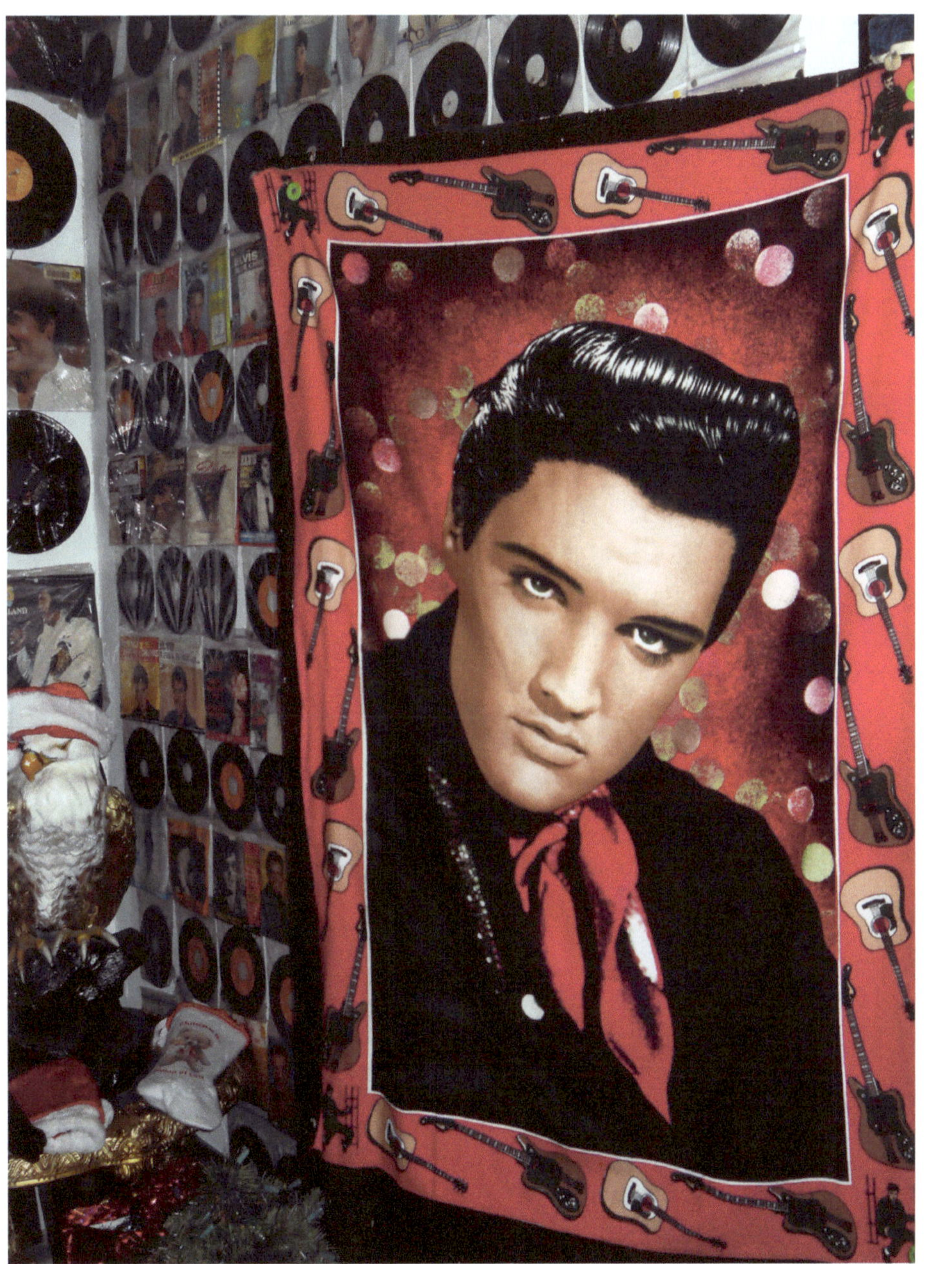

Stand-up Elvis

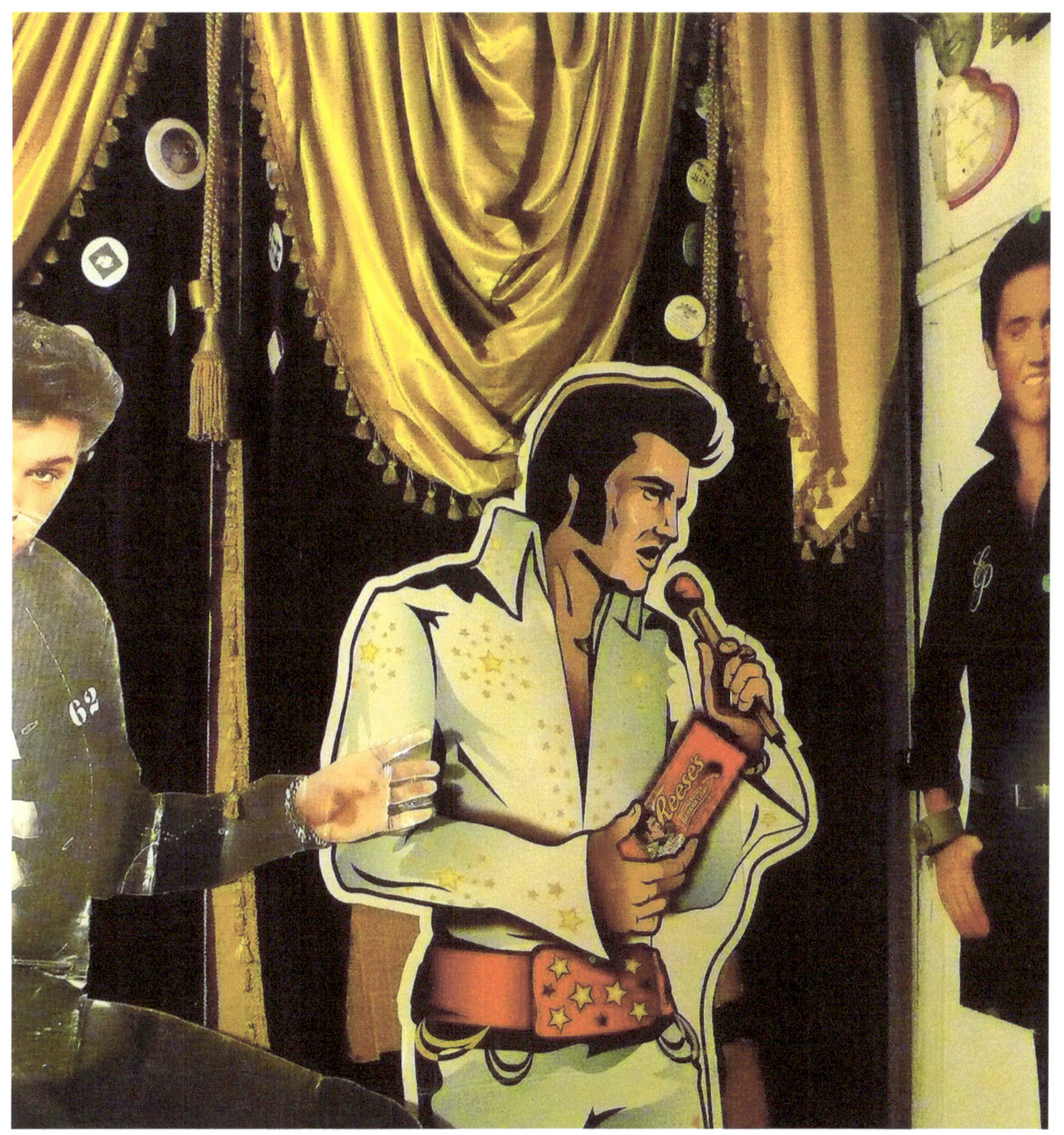

62
Reese's

Naked Lightbulbs

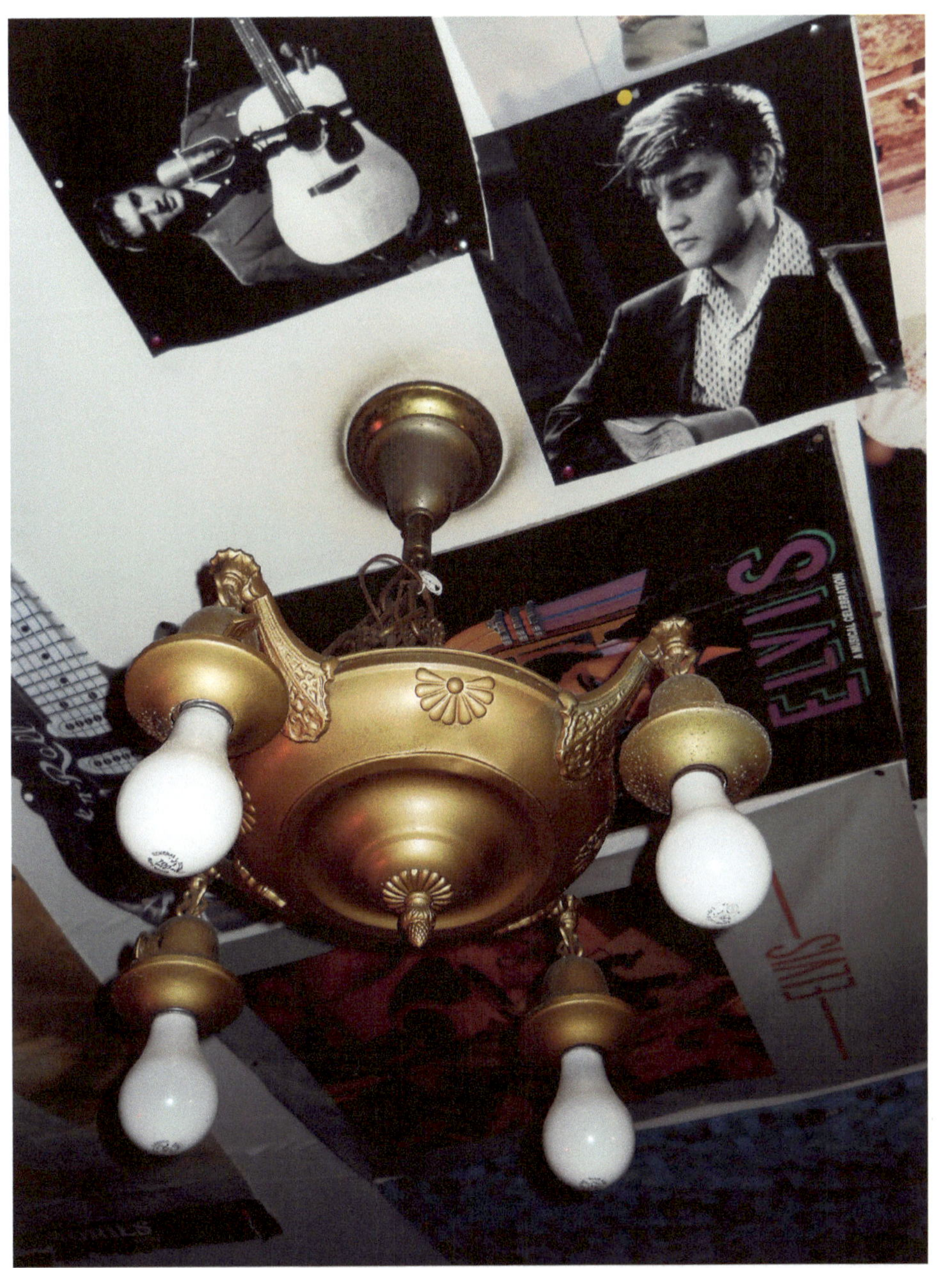

ELVIS
A MUSICAL CELEBRATION
ELVIS

Paul in Middle Age

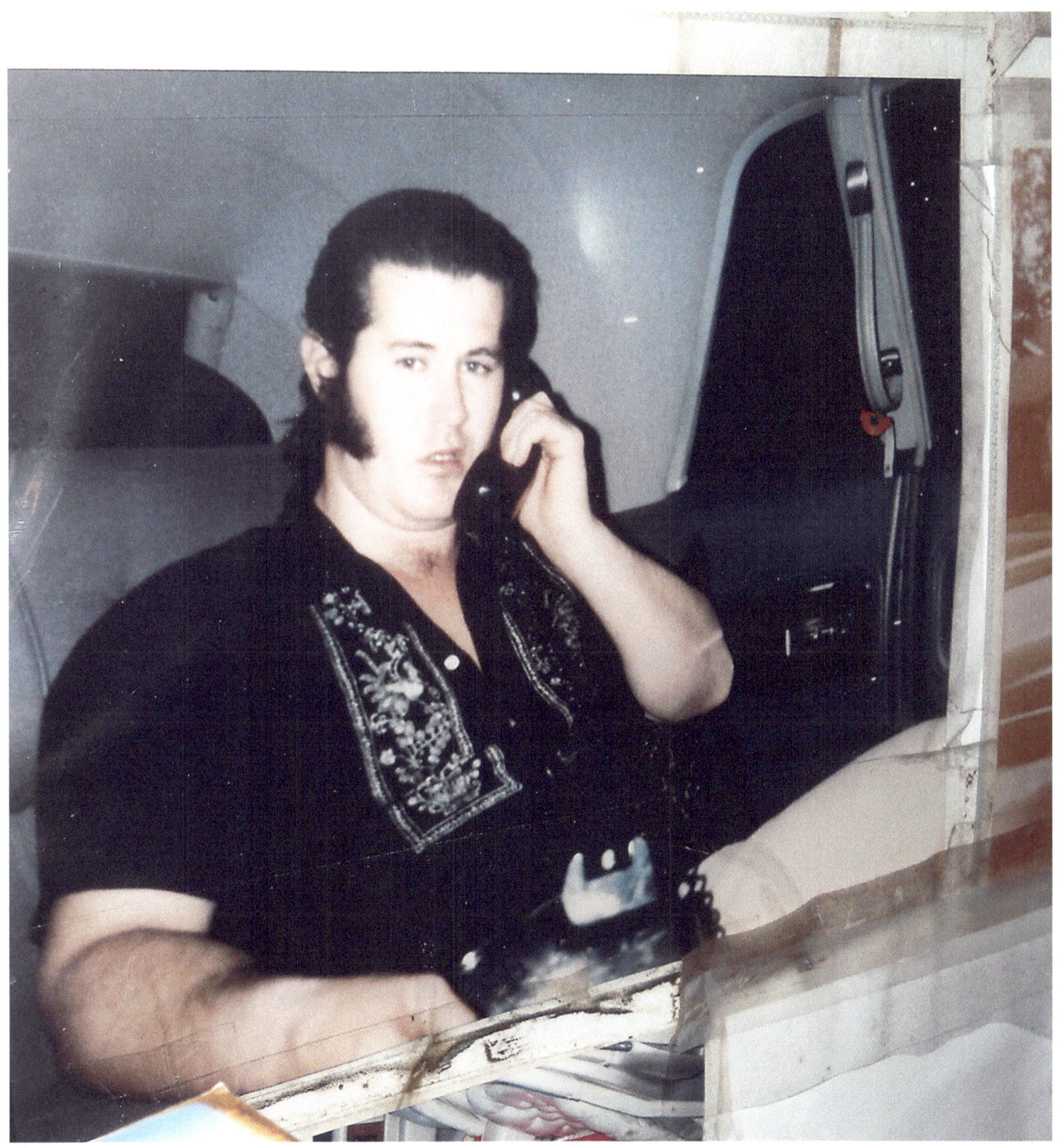

Mantelpiece Elvis

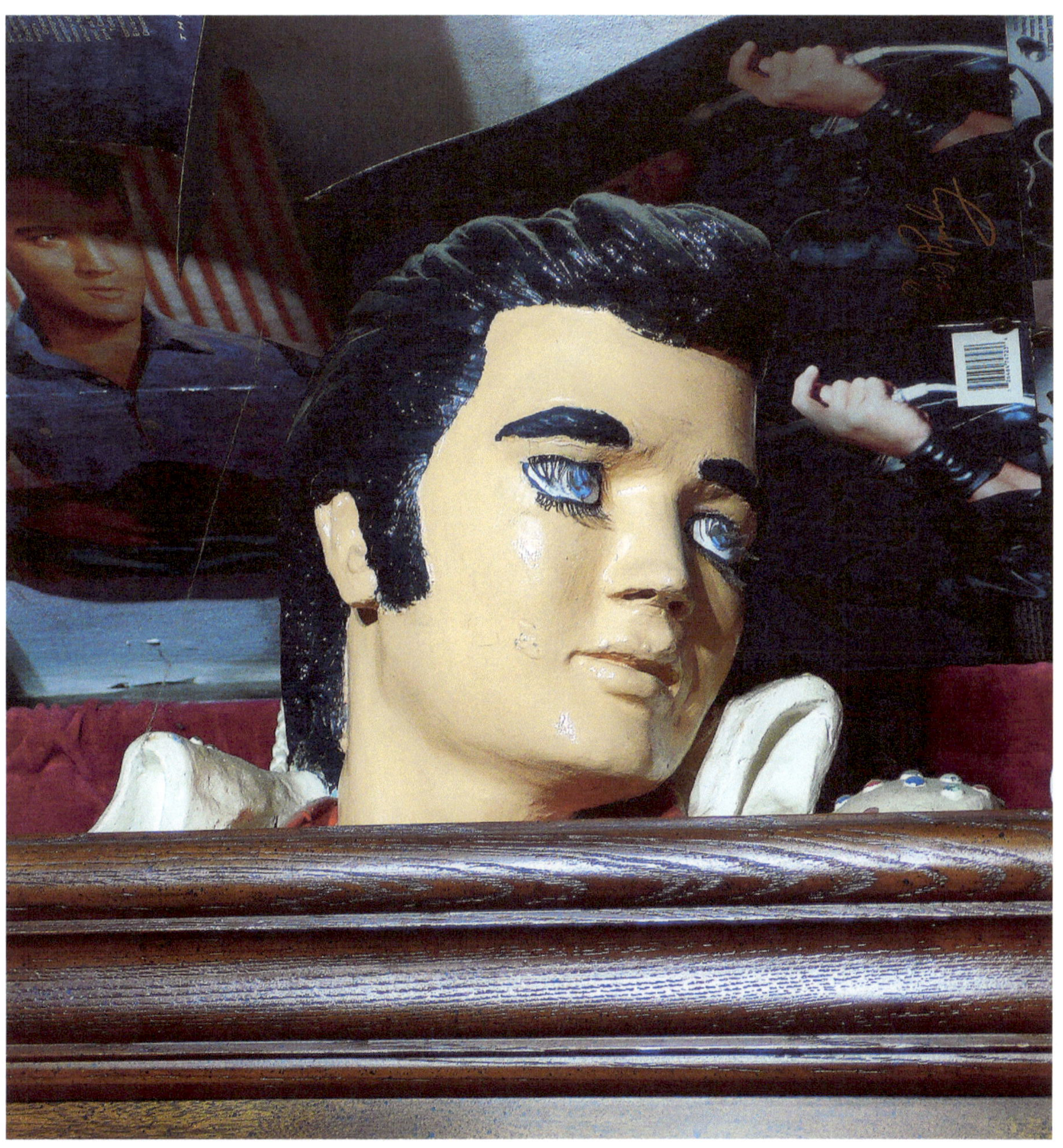

Christmas with Elvis

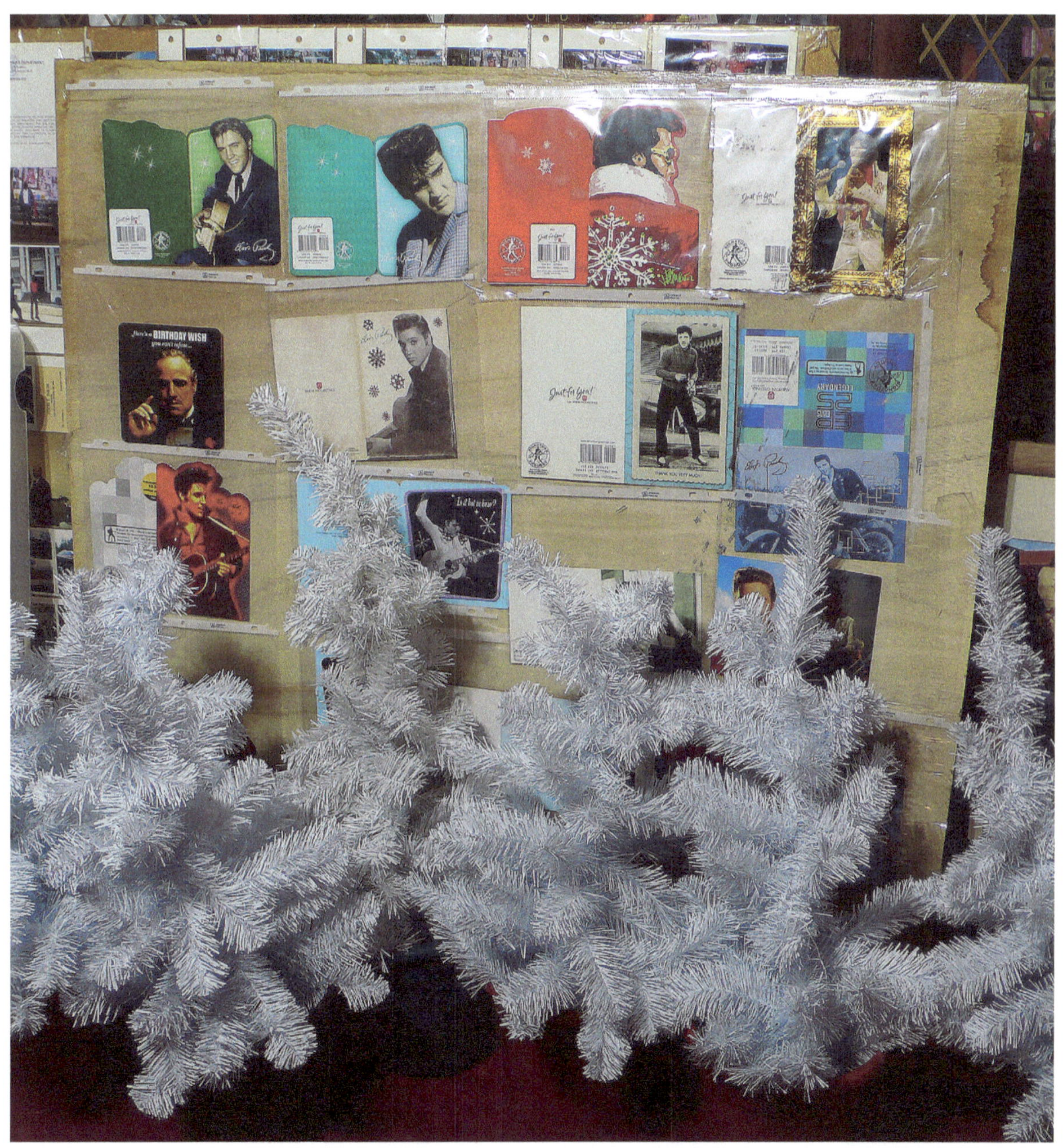

Graceland Too Candelabra

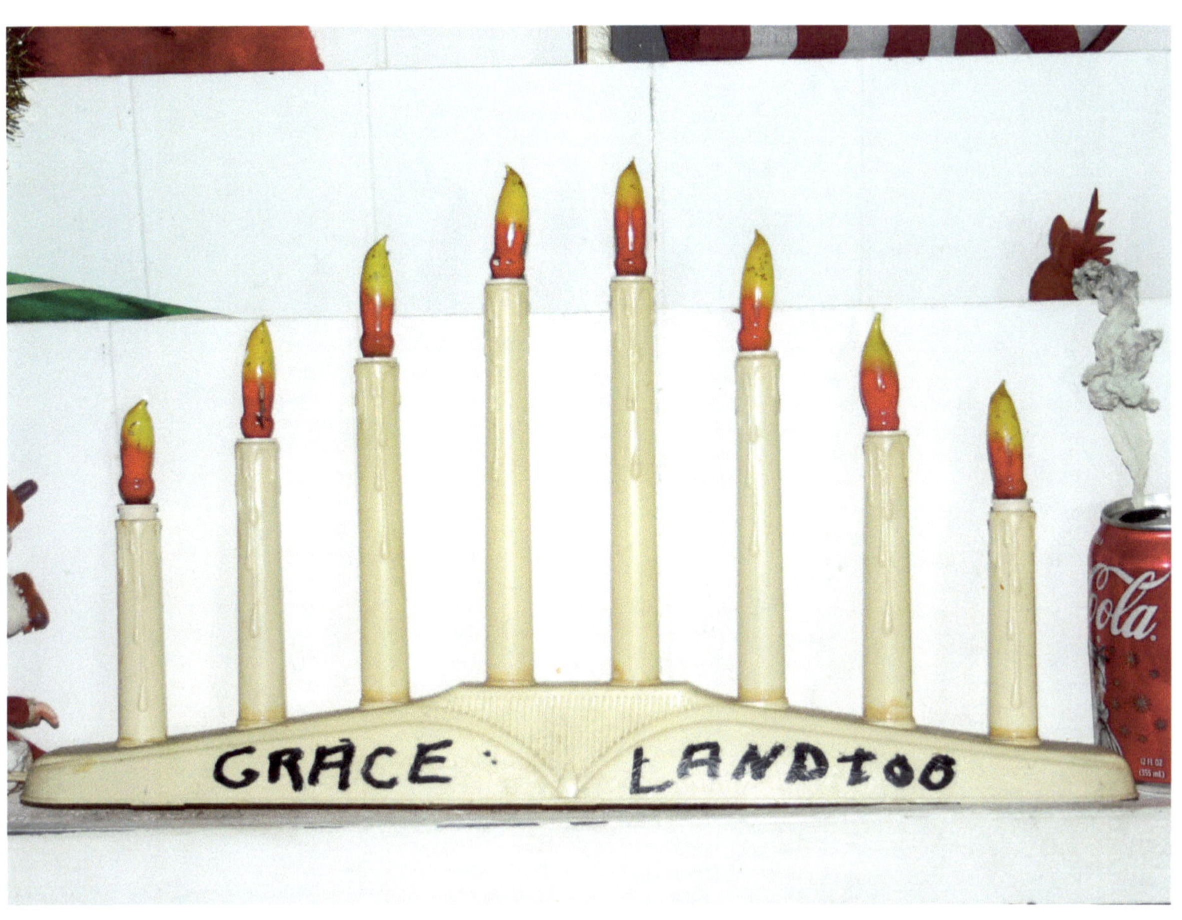

GRACE · LANDtoo

Alarm Clock Elvis

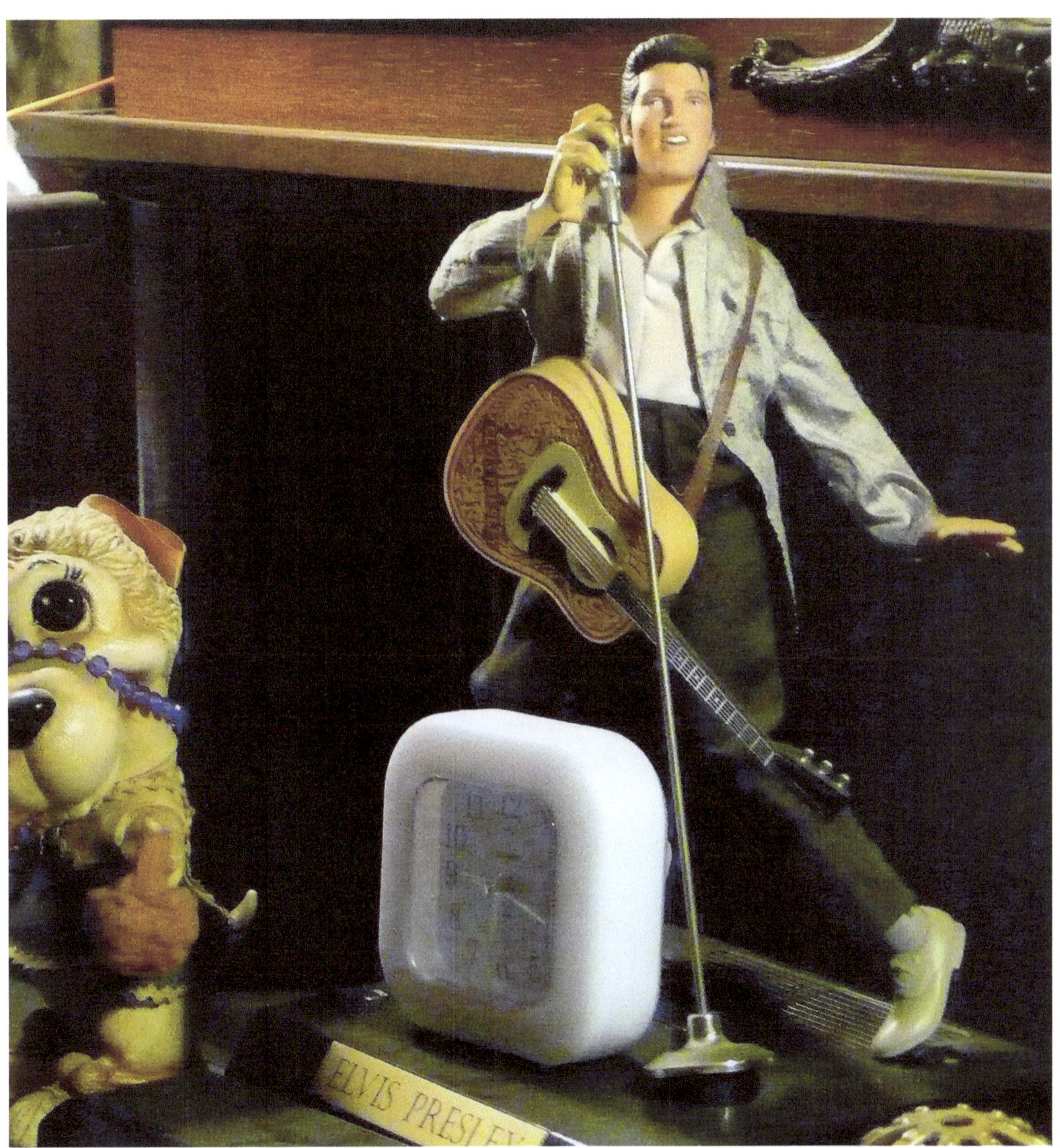

ELVIS PRESLEY

Ceiling Clutter

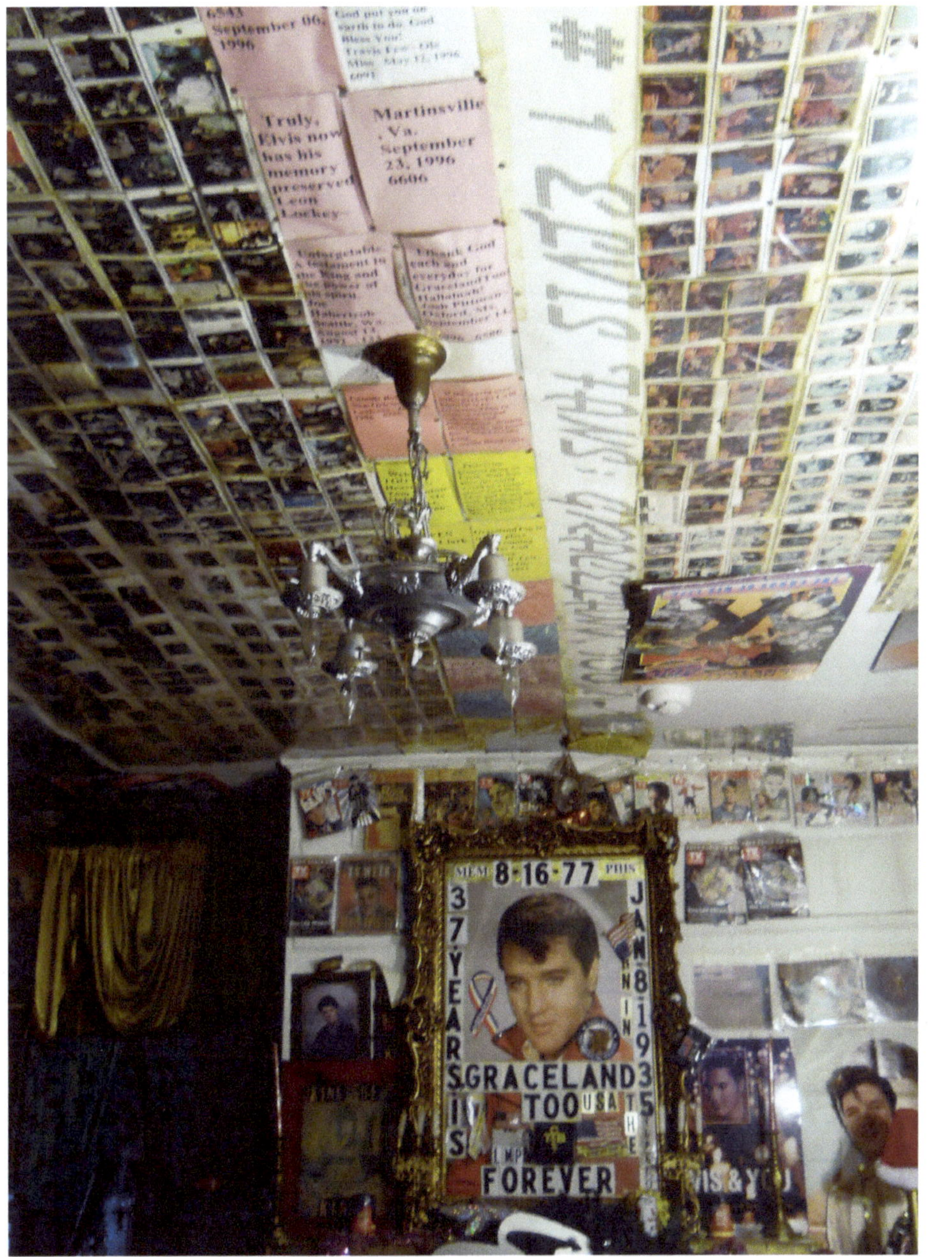

Leather Jacket for Lifetime Members

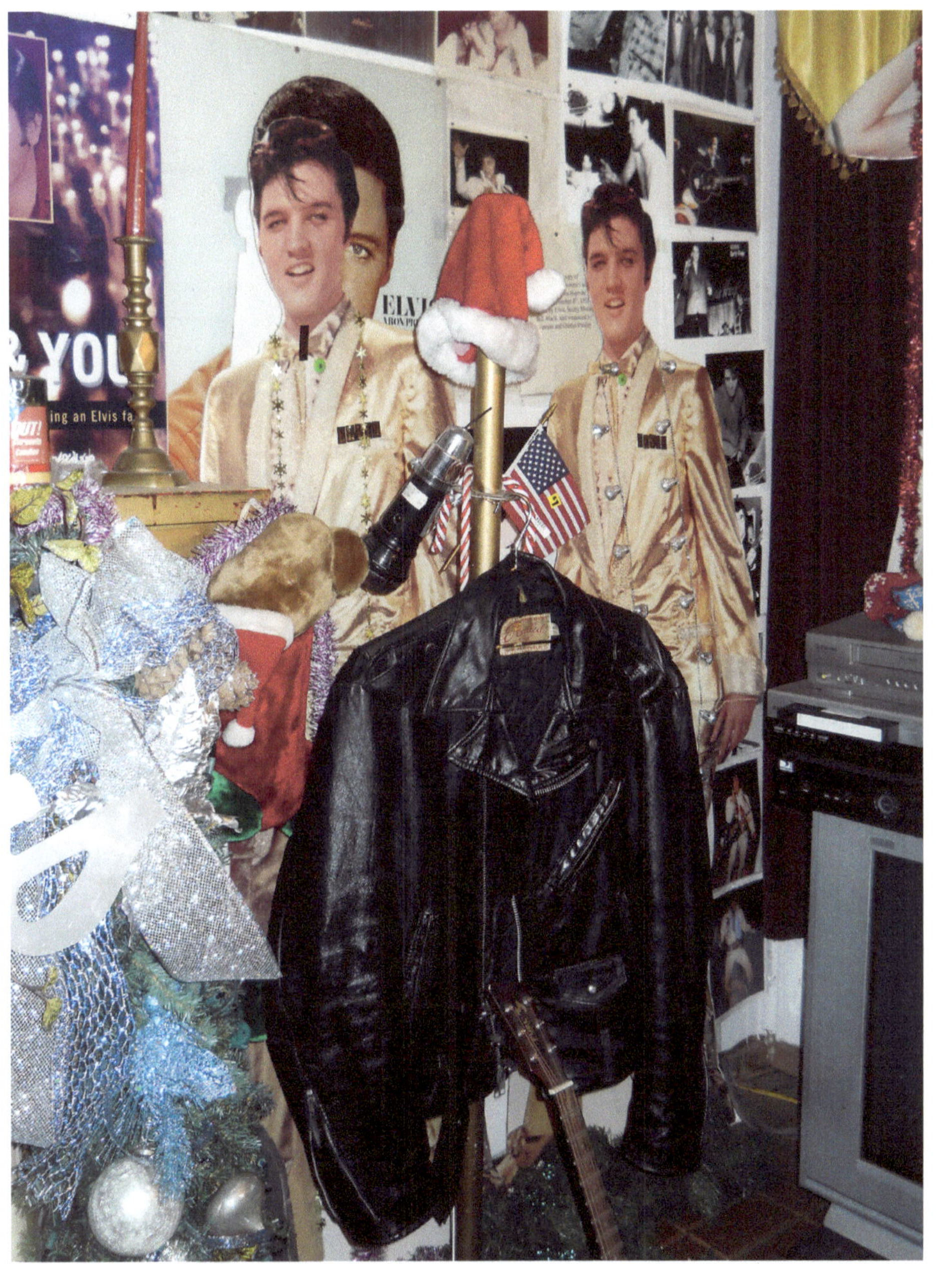

Lifetime Member Wall

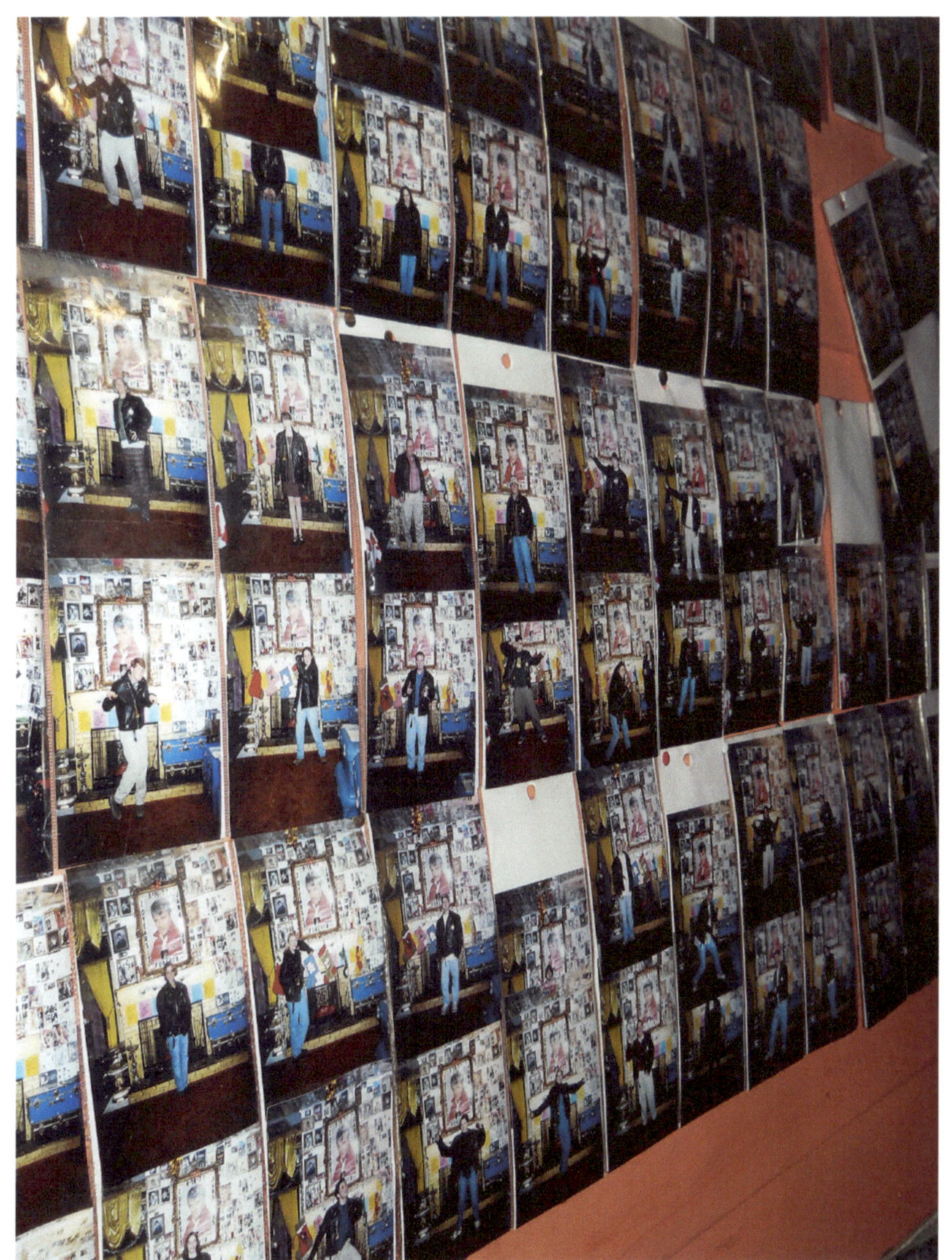

Curtains

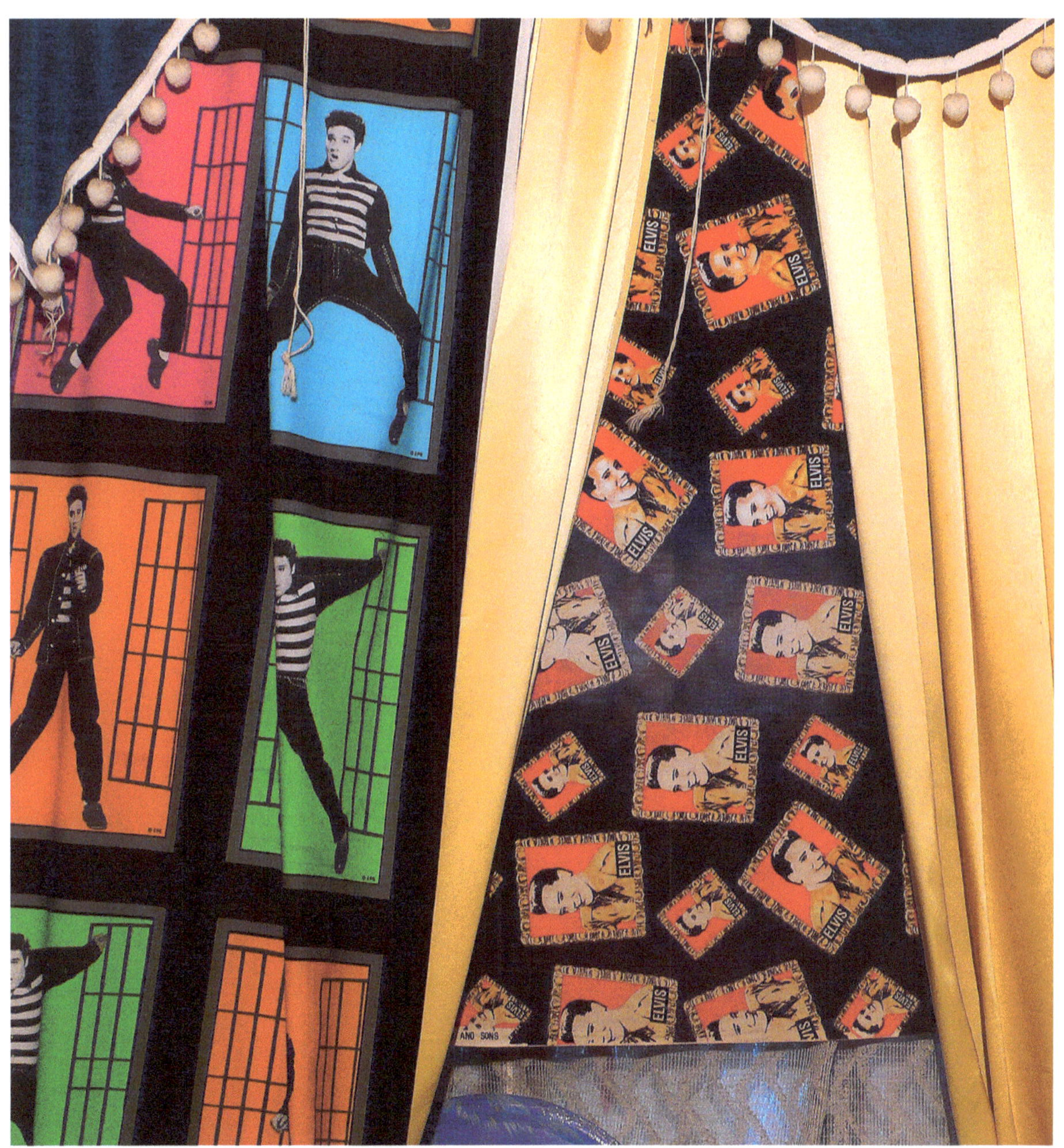

ELVIS
ELVIS
ELVIS
ELVIS
ELVIS
ELVIS
ELVIS
AND SONS

Paul's Shrine to Elvis

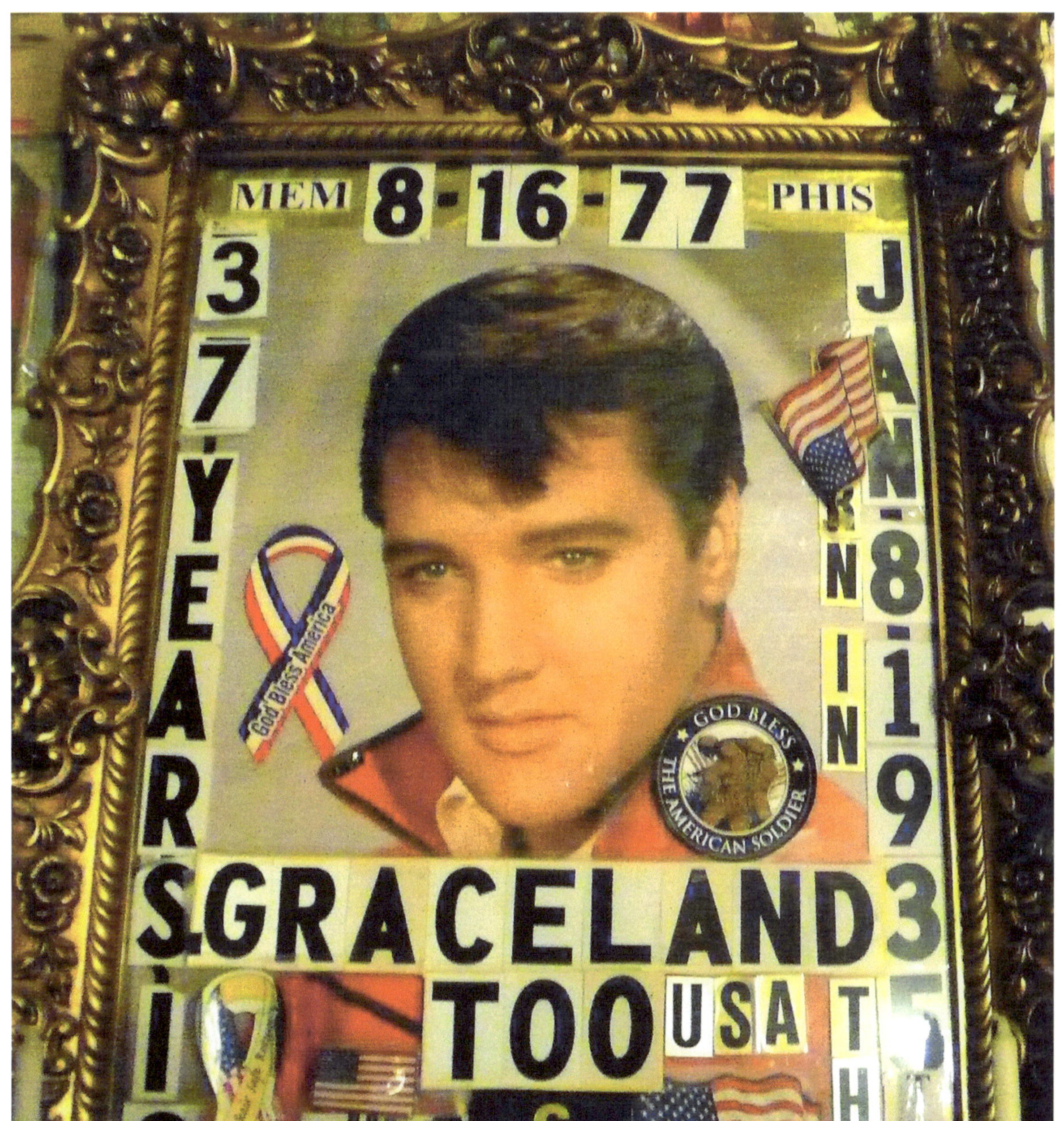
MEM 8-16-77 PHIS
37 YEARS
GRACELAND TOO
JAN 8-19-35
USA
God Bless America
GOD BLESS THE AMERICAN SOLDIER

All Stitched Up

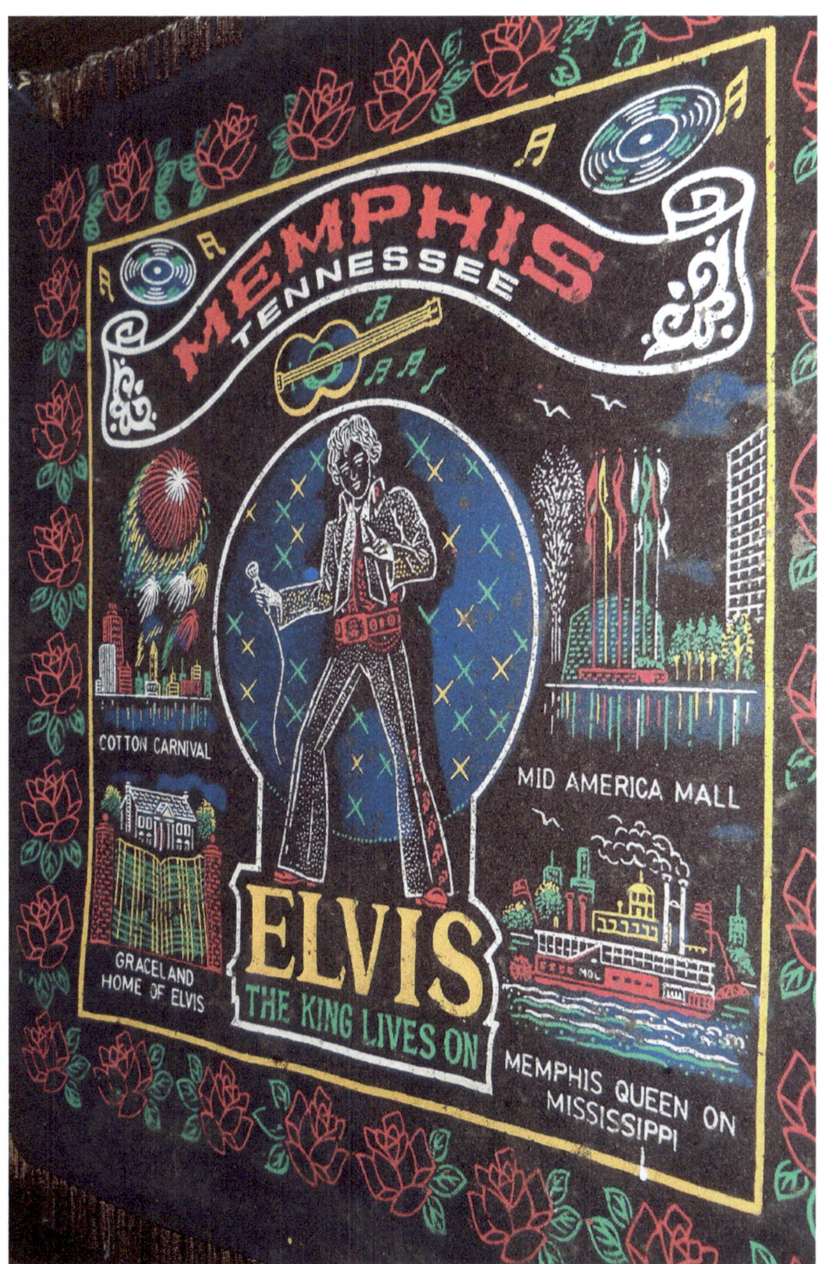
MEMPHIS
TENNESSEE
COTTON CARNIVAL
MID AMERICA MALL
GRACELAND
HOME OF ELVIS
ELVIS
THE KING LIVES ON
MEMPHIS QUEEN ON
MISSISSIPPI

This Is Elvis

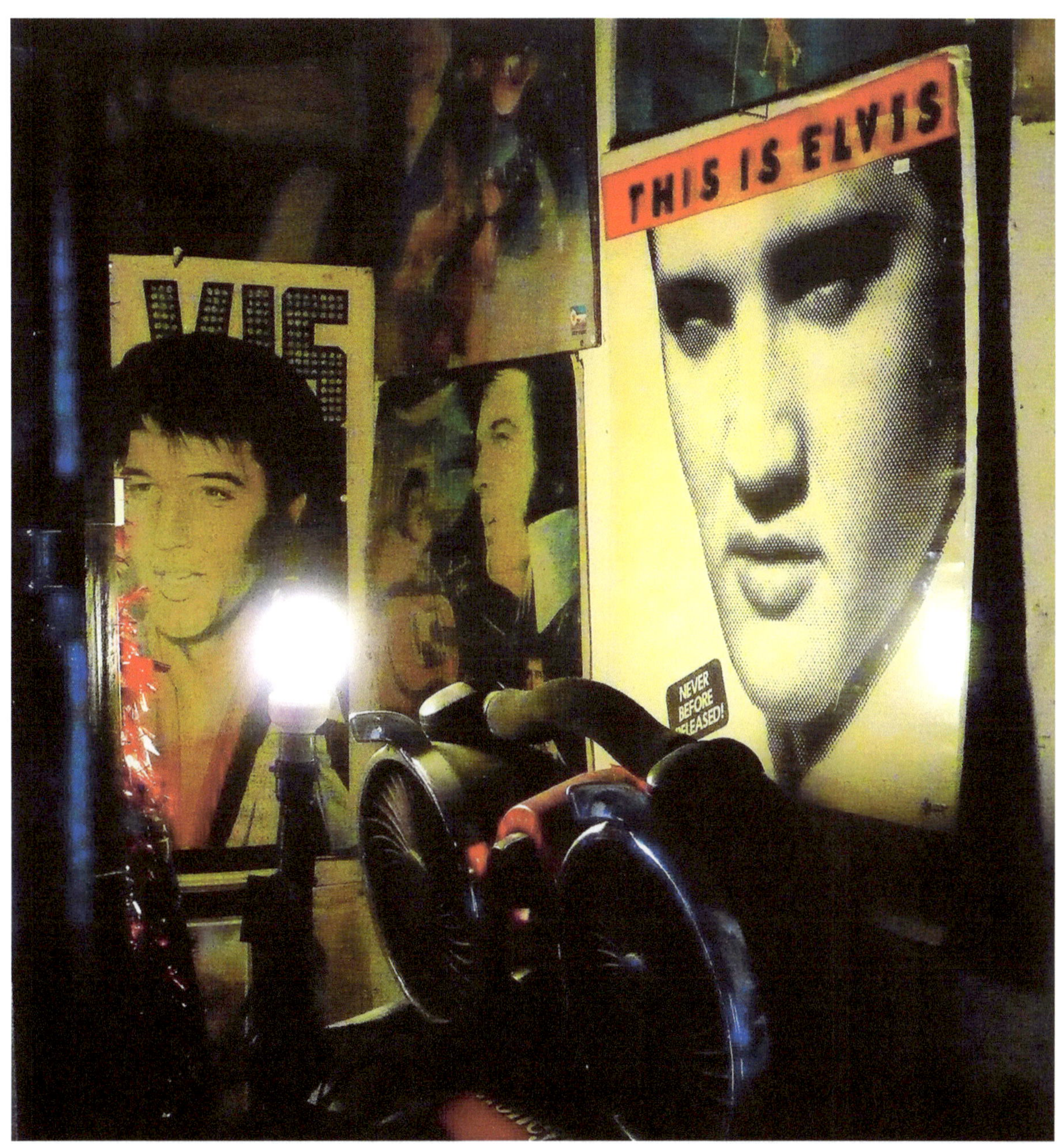
THIS IS ELVIS
VIS
NEVER BEFORE RELEASED!

Bag Elvis

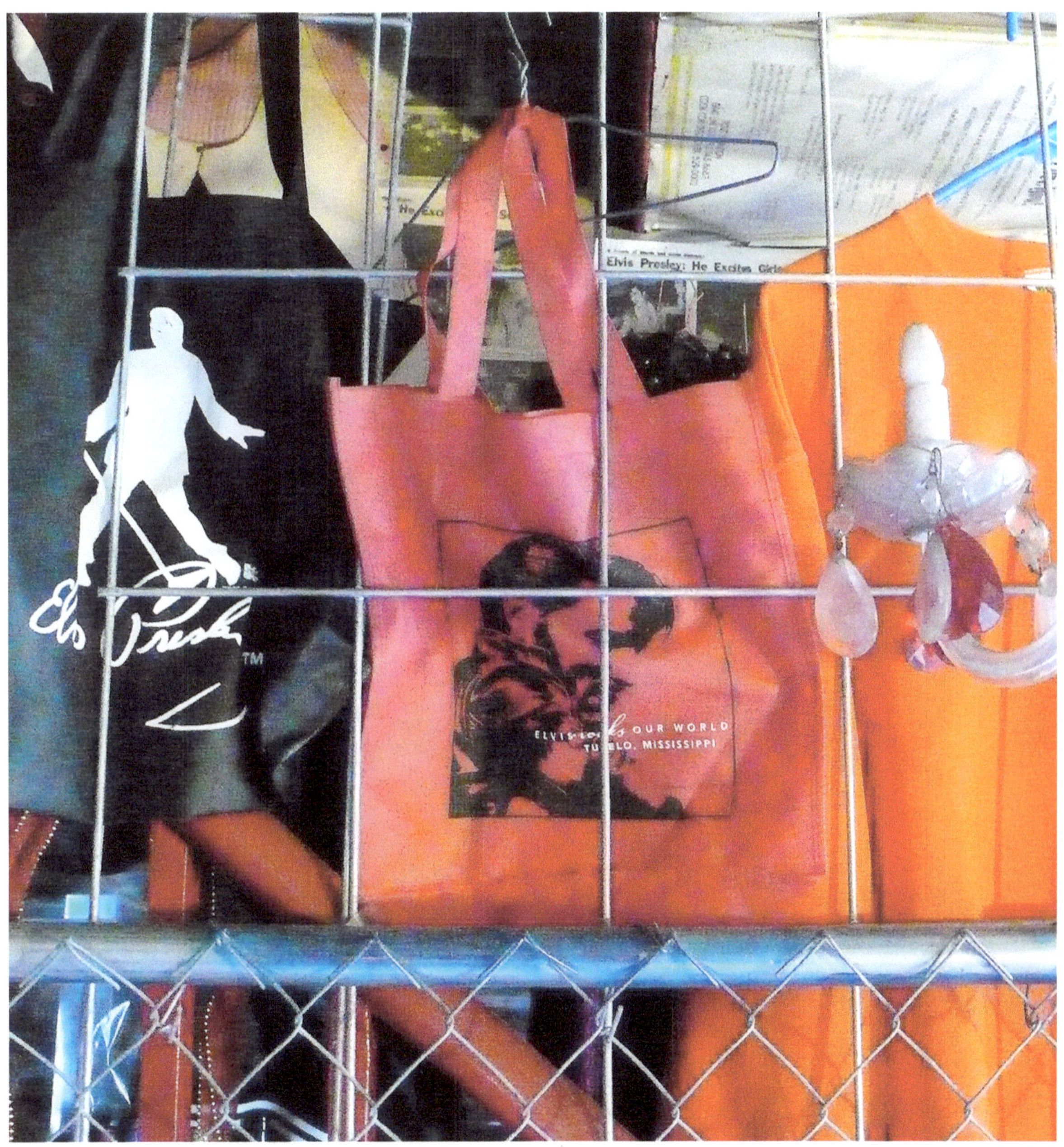

Elvis Presley: He Excites Girls
ELVIS ROCKS OUR WORLD
TUPELO, MISSISSIPPI

Moody Blue

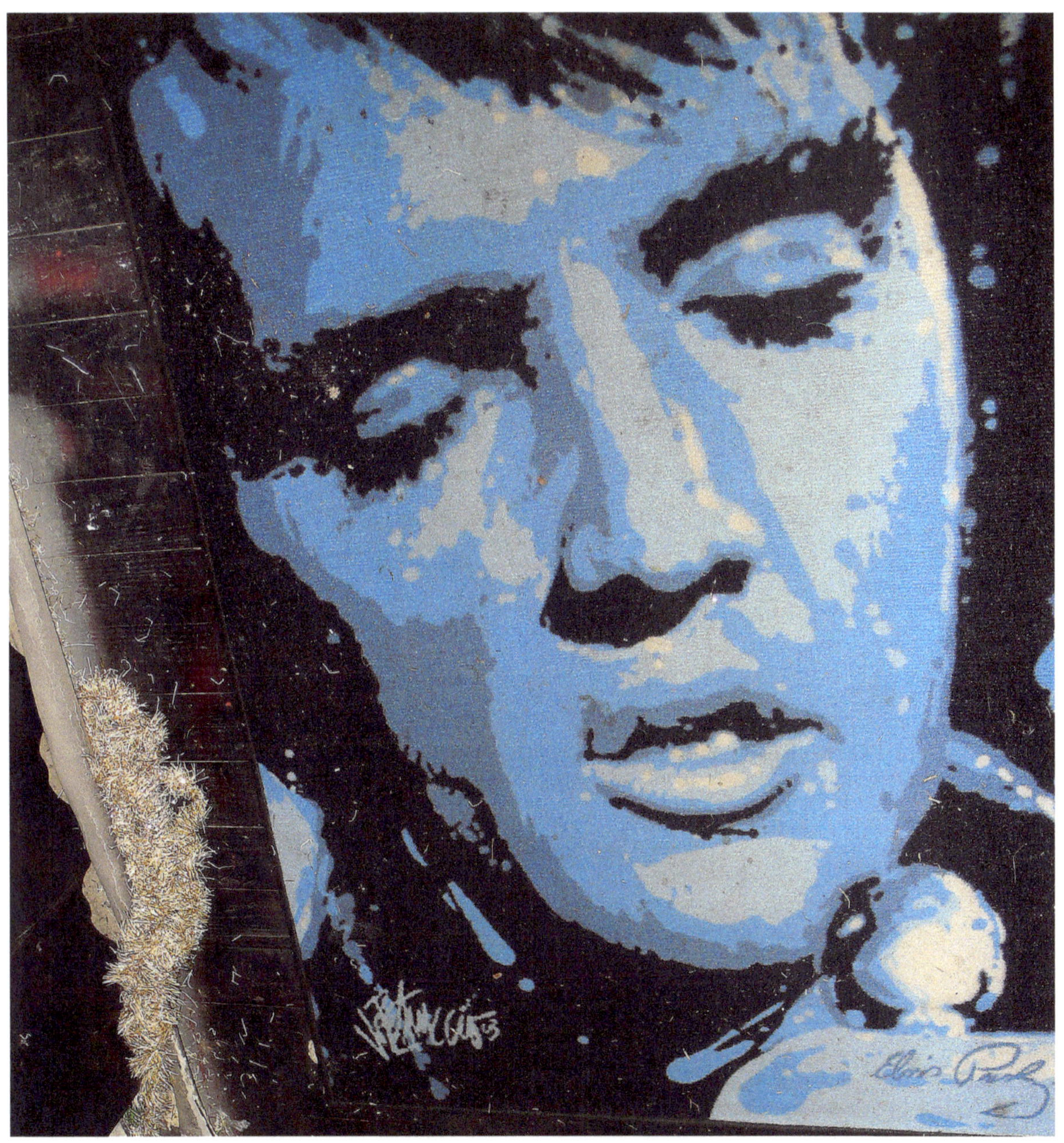

Jailhouse Rock Electric Chair

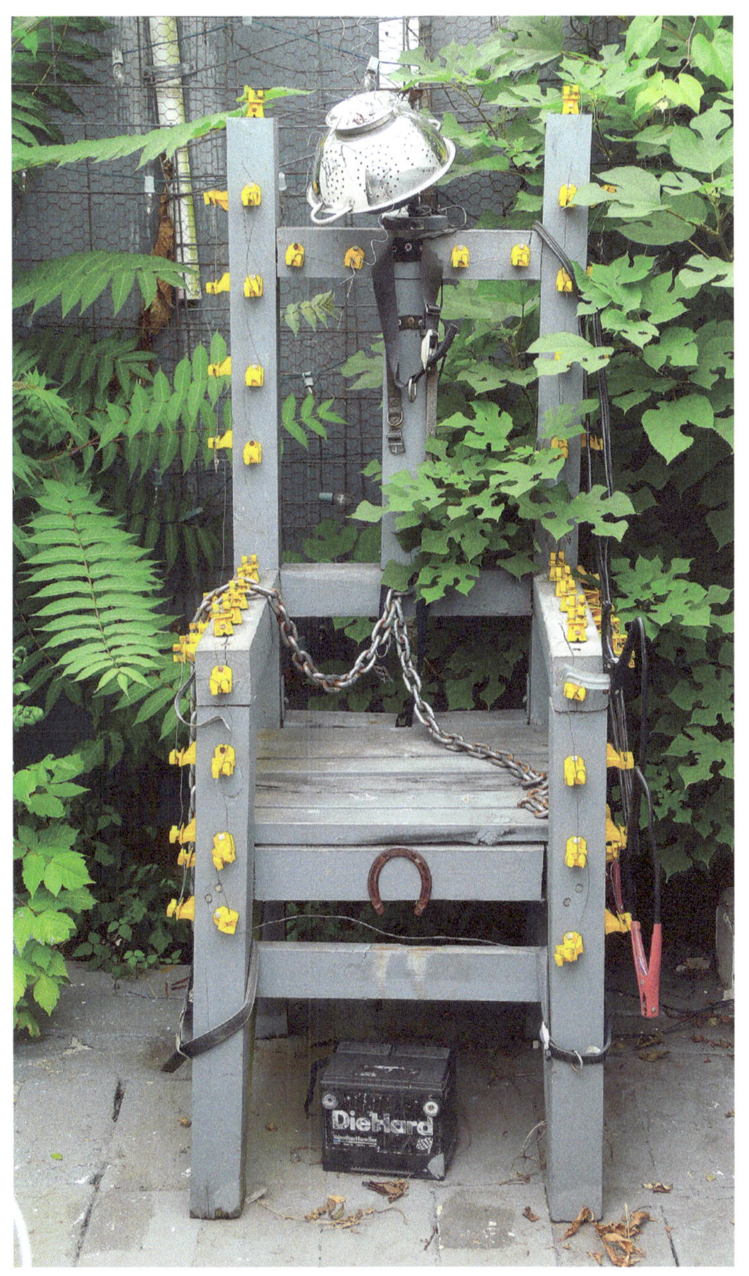

Jailhouse Rock Prisoner

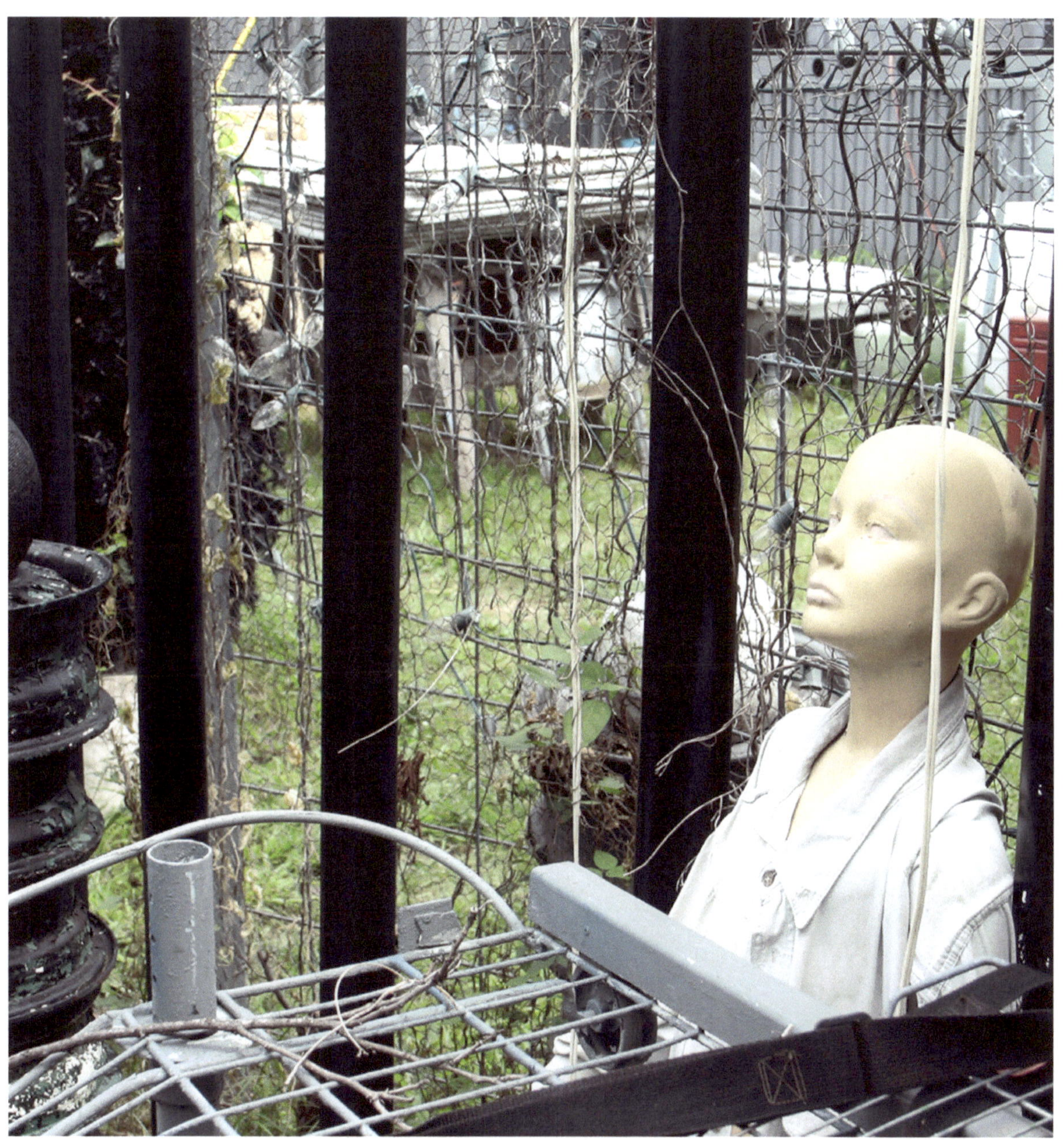

Blue Jaws

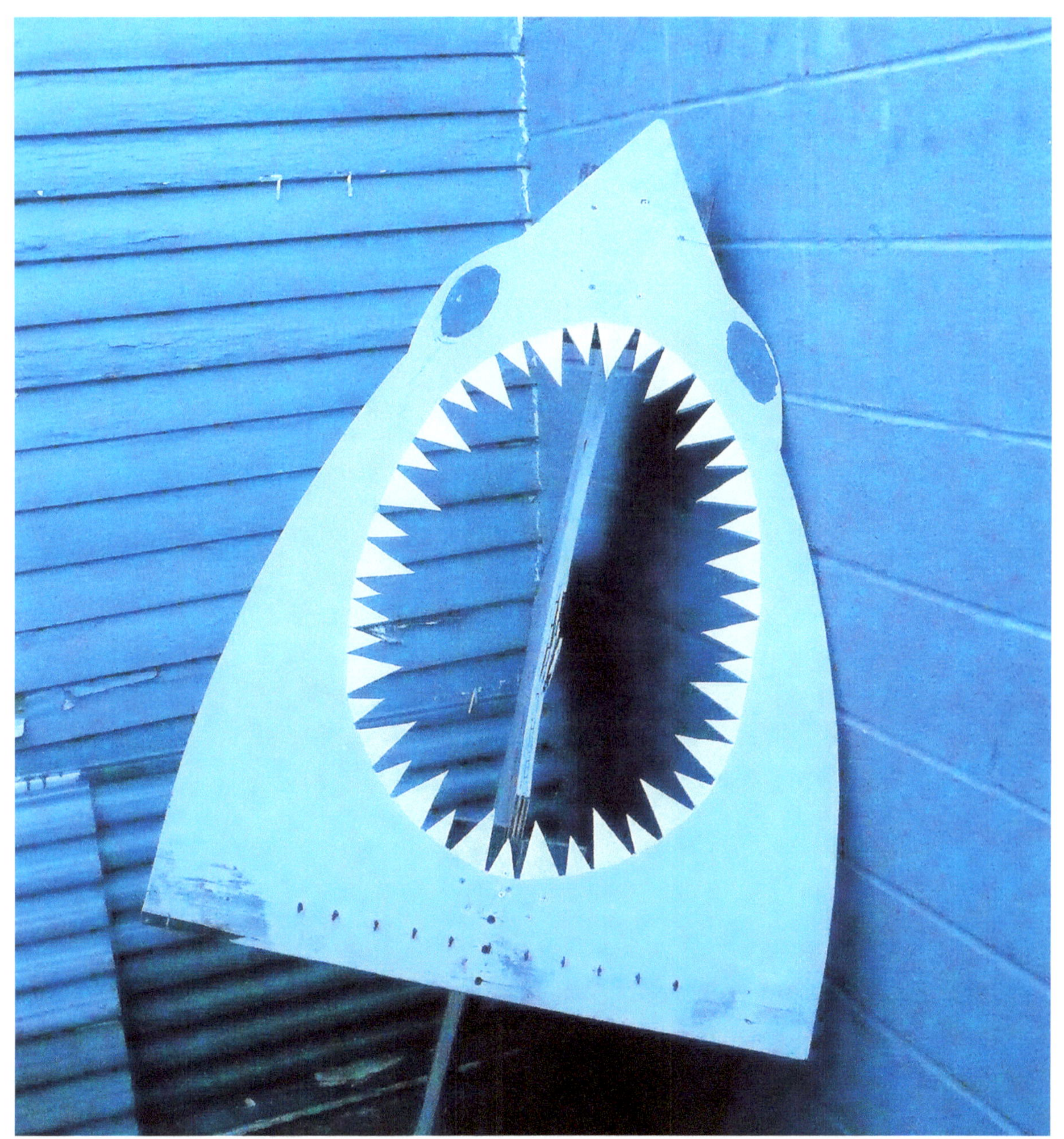

Pink Limo

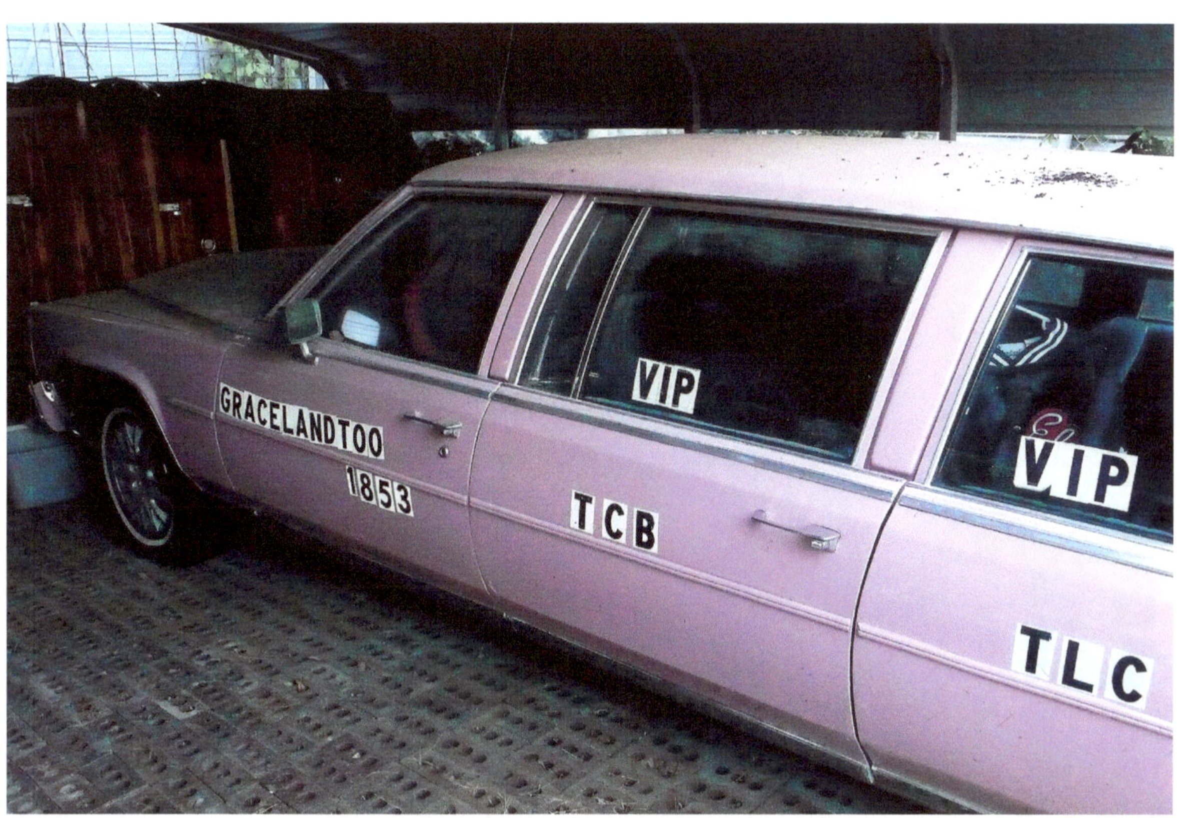
GRACELANDTOO
1853
TCB
VIP
VIP
TLC

Tributes to Paul

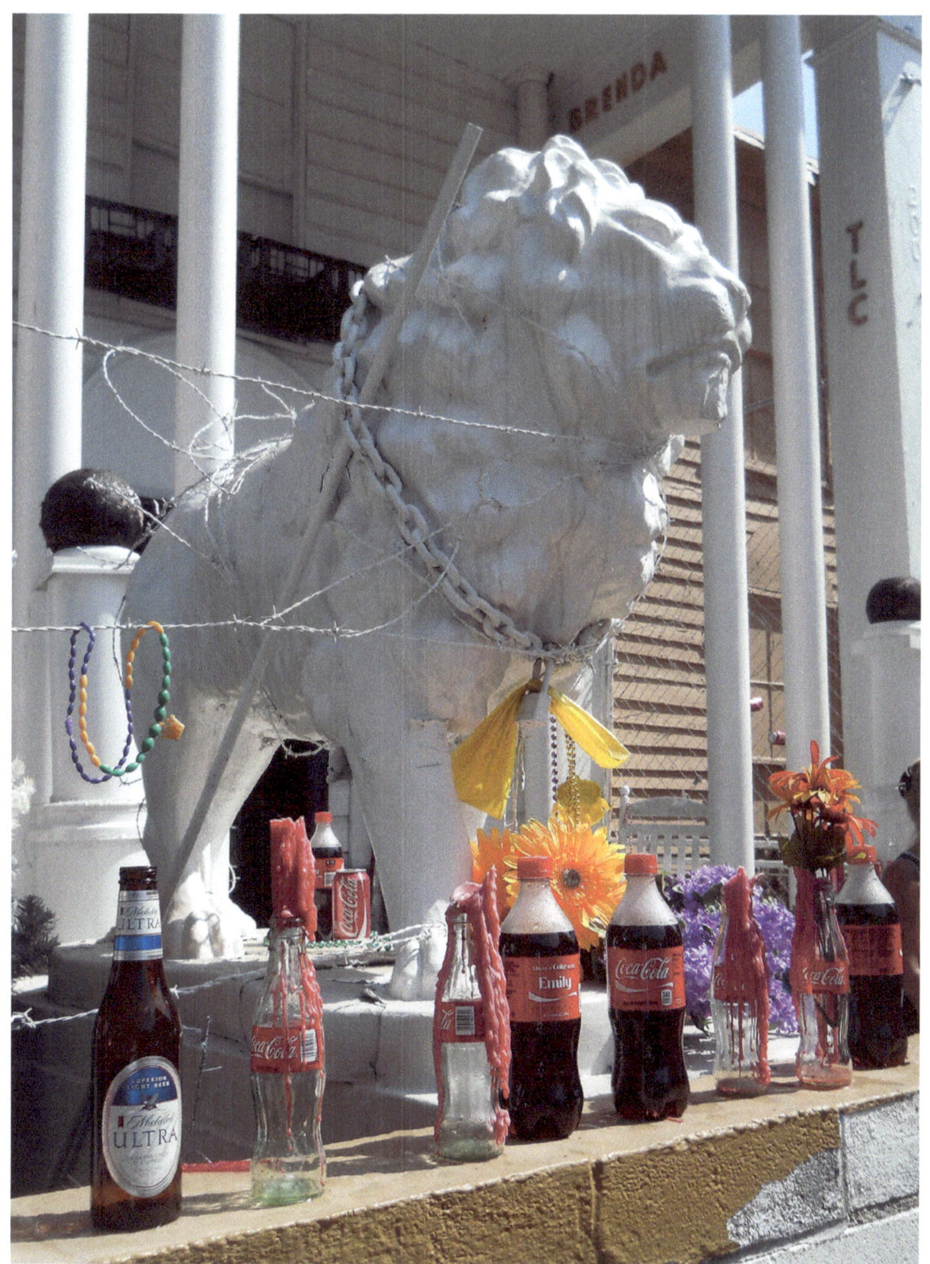

Cokes in Chain Link

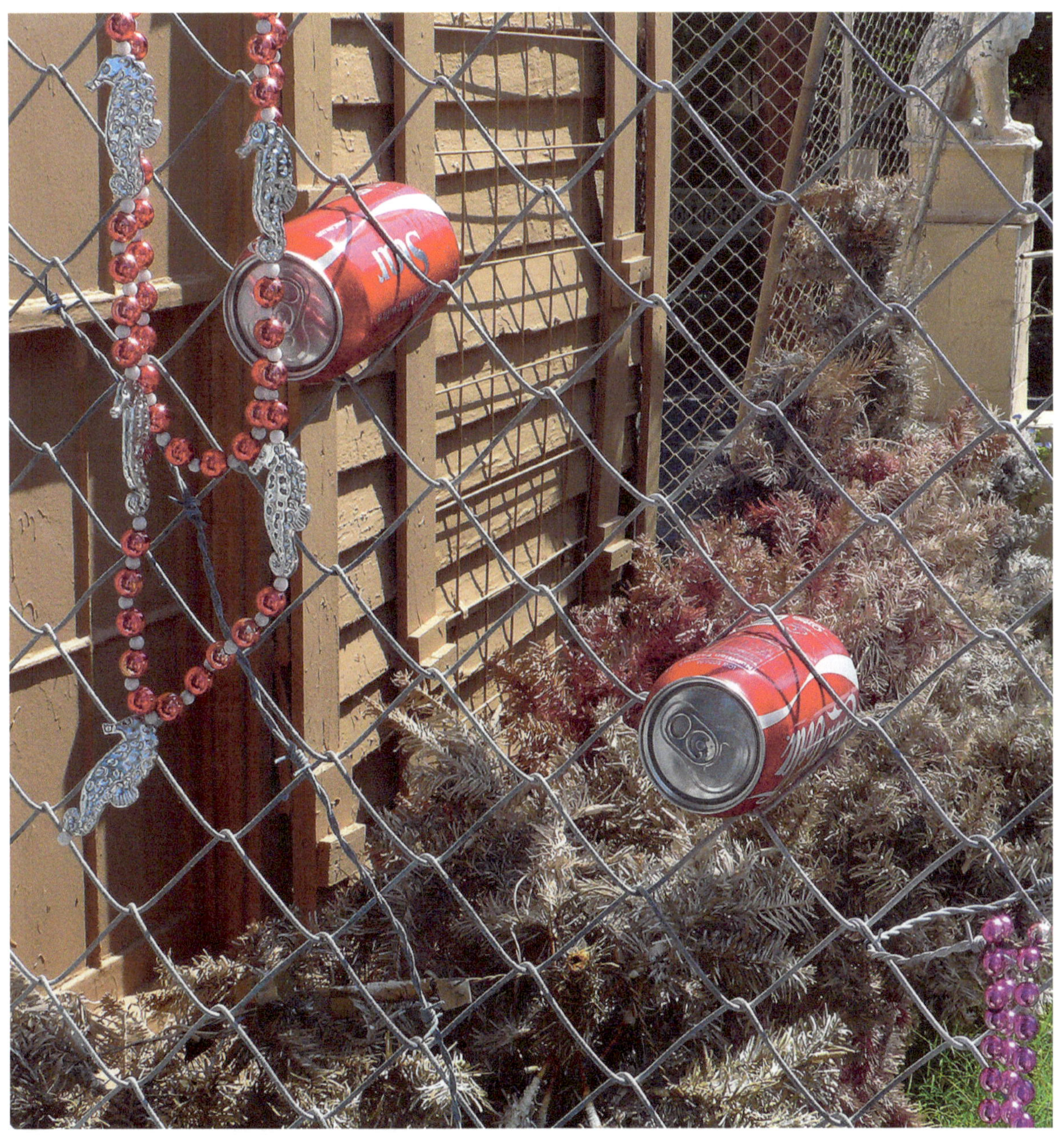

Final Tour Day

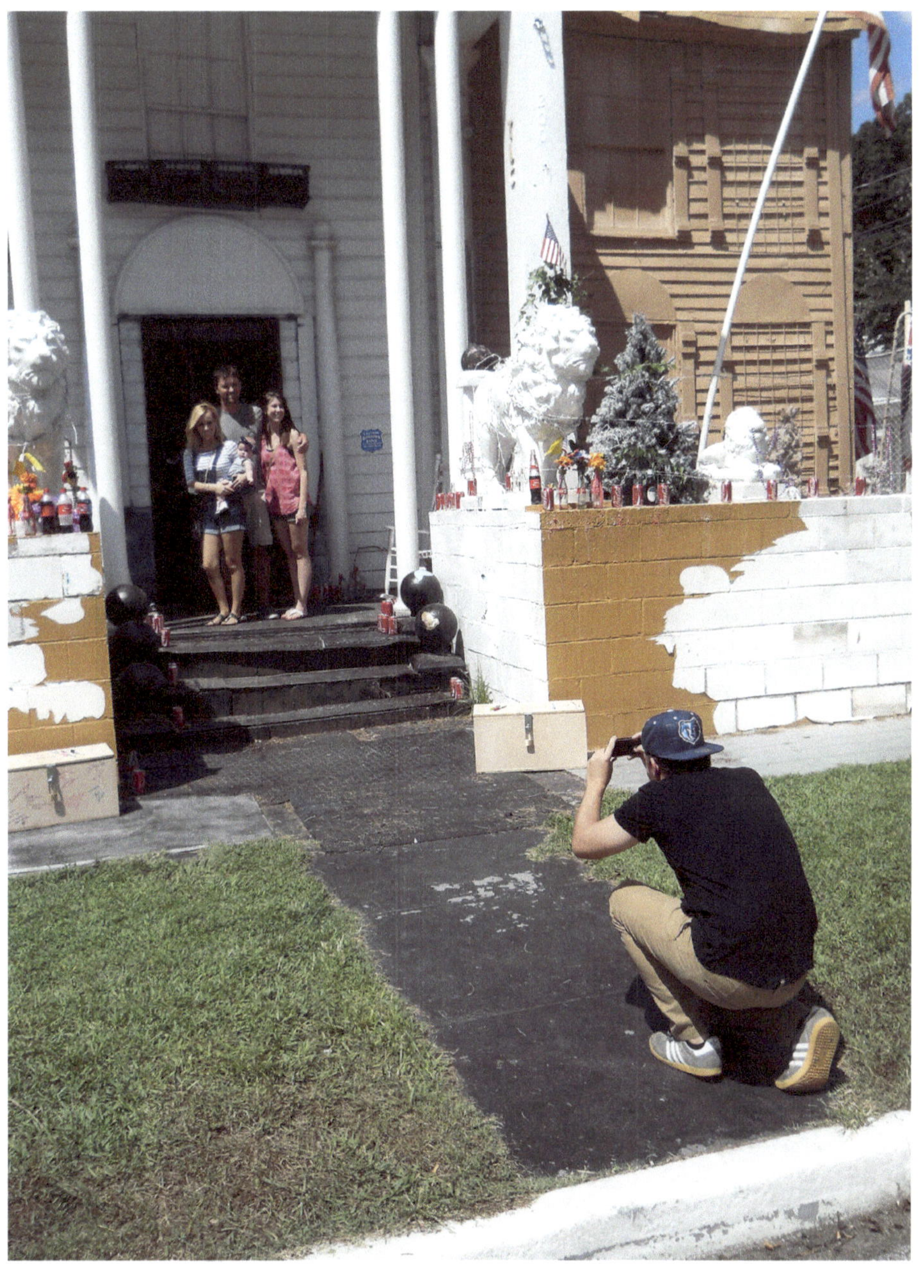

Photo Credits

Cover image: Darrin Devault

Pages 5-7: Darrin Devault

Page 9: Darrin Devault

Page 11: Tom Graves

Page 13: Darrin Devault

Page 15: Darrin Devault

Page 17: Darrin Devault

Page 19: Tom Graves

Page 21: Tom Graves

Page 23: Tom Graves

Page 25: Darrin Devault

Page 27: Tom Graves

Page 29: Darrin Devault

Page 31: Darrin Devault

Page 33: Tom Graves

Page 35: Tom Graves

Page 37: Darrin Devault

Page 39: Tom Graves

Page 41: Darrin Devault

Page 43: Darrin Devault

Page 45: Darrin Devault

Page 47: Tom Graves

Page 49: Tom Graves

Page 51: Darrin Devault

Page 53: Tom Graves

Page 55: Tom Graves

Page 57: Tom Graves

Page 59: Tom Graves

Page 61: Darrin Devault

Page 63: Tom Graves

Page 65: Tom Graves

Page 67: Darrin Devault

Page 69: Tom Graves

Page 71: Darrin Devault

About the Photographers

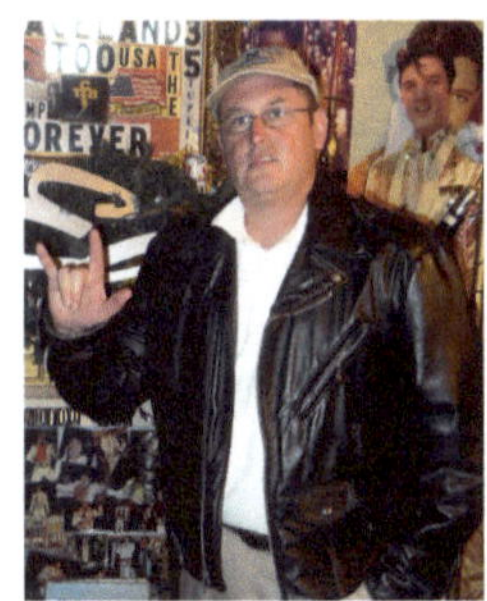

Darrin Devault is a book publisher and photographer based in Memphis and Townsend, Tennessee. He also is a journalism professor at the University of Memphis.

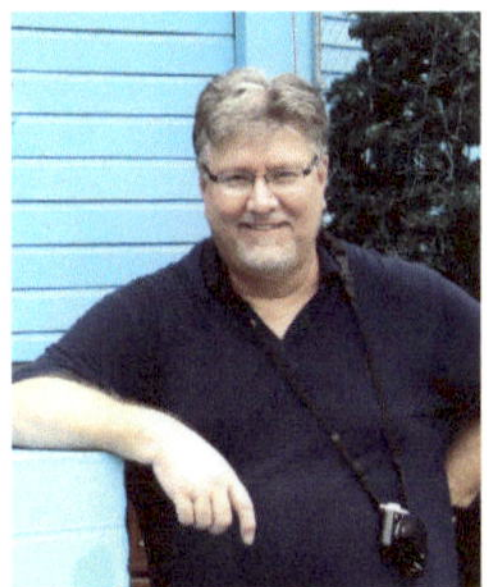

Tom Graves is an author, book publisher, and photographer based in Memphis. He also is an English and journalism professor at LeMoyne-Owen College.

Devault and Graves are the founding partners of The Devault-Graves Agency in Memphis. They currently publish under two imprints: Devault-Graves Digital Editions and Chalk Line Books.

www.devault-gravesagency.com

Acknowledgments

Shari MacLeod and Brenda Young, Daughters of Paul B. MacLeod

The Citizens of Holly Springs and Marshall County, Mississippi

Phillip K. Knecht, Attorney at Law, Knecht Law Firm, PLLC

Rev. Bruce D. McMillan, Rector, Christ Episcopal Church, Holly Springs

Tim Liddy, Alderman at Large, City of Holly Springs

Lakisha Buffington, Executive Director, Holly Springs Tourism & Recreation Bureau

Annie Moffitt, Friend of Paul B. MacLeod

Suzann Williams, Friend of Paul B. MacLeod